T0265573

Millionaire Habits

Millionaire Habits

How to Achieve Financial Independence, Retire Early, and Make a Difference by Focusing on Yourself First

Steve Adcock

WILEY

Published by John Wiley & Sons, Inc., Hoboken, New Jersey.
Published simultaneously in Canada.

For general information on our other products and services or for technical support, please contact our Customer Care Department within the United States at (800) 762-2974, outside the United States at (317) 572-3993 or fax (317) 572-4002.

Wiley also publishes its books in a variety of electronic formats. Some content that appears in print may not be available in electronic formats. For more information about Wiley products, visit our web site at www.wiley.com.

Library of Congress Cataloging-in-Publication Data

Names: Adcock, Steve (Entrepreneur), author.
Title: Millionaire habits : how to achieve financial independence, retire
  early, and make a difference by focusing on yourself first / Steve
  Adcock.
Description: Hoboken, New Jersey : Wiley, [2024]
Identifiers: LCCN 2023041010 (print) | LCCN 2023041011 (ebook) | ISBN
  9781394197293 (cloth) | ISBN 9781394197316 (adobe pdf) | ISBN
  9781394197309 (epub)
Subjects: LCSH: Finance, Personal. | Early retirement.
Classification: LCC HG179 .A343 2024 (print) | LCC HG179 (ebook) | DDC
  332.024—dc23/eng/20230920
LC record available at https://lccn.loc.gov/2023041010
LC ebook record available at https://lccn.loc.gov/2023041011

Cover Design: Wiley
Author Photo: Courtesy of the Author
SKY100660123_111523

Contents

Introduction

Nobody ever got rich by making excuses. Not me. Not you. Nobody. Excuses don't build wealth. If they did, everyone would be rich, wouldn't they?

There is no shortage of excuses.

"I don't have time!"

"I'm not smart enough!"

"I didn't grow up rich!"

Listen up, buttercup: I'm not here to tell you everything is going to be okay and that if you believe in yourself and sing kumbaya around a campfire, great things will happen.

That's not how life works. Yes, believing in yourself is great, but **putting actions behind that belief** is how we achieve amazing things, such as becoming a millionaire. A hope without action is nothing but a wish. Millionaires don't get rich by wishing.

Throughout this book, I will respond to those three excuses with simple answers:

"Yes, you do!"
"Yes, you are!"
"Who cares?"

We all have the same 24 hours in a day. The problem isn't having enough time, being smart enough, or growing up with rich parents. Those are excuses. Thousands become millionaires without inheritances, having rich parents, and getting straight As in school. There is no reason why you can't become one of them.

Growing up, I suffered from a learning disability. My school district forced me to take a "Basic Skills" class through middle school because I didn't learn as fast as my classmates, affectionately referring to me as "learning disabled." The Basic Skills class gave me extra time and help to get my homework done during the school day instead of taking another "real" class. Basic Skills was where they put all the "disabled" kids.

Apparently, I had a disability because my learning style was different. It took me more time to grasp concepts, especially in math. I struggled to understand ideas that other kids seemed to pick up on the first try. And let's just say that I wasn't exactly a straight-A student, either. I excelled in science classes, but in every other class, I was happy with a B. By the end of high school, I graduated with a solid 2.7 GPA.

But you know what? It didn't matter. My wife Courtney and I still became millionaires in our early 30s without graduating at the top of my class and attending a prestigious college. I never got an inheritance. I didn't even start my own business. We worked regular nine-to-five jobs, saved and invested our money, and it grew.

In other words, I'm telling you that I wasn't a gifted student. For most of my young life, I didn't consider myself smart. But I still managed to achieve a life I never thought possible. I'm here to tell you that you can, too. If you live in the industrialized world, almost anything is possible.

There's no magic in our story. No get-rich-quick hacks. Everything I did to build wealth anyone can do. It starts with developing repeatable habits that attract money and success. That's right, most millionaires don't chase money.

They attract it.

Earning a high salary enabled us to retire in our 30s; not everyone can do that. Don't compare our retirement age with yours because that's not the point.

Instead, take the concepts from this book, implement them in your lives, and retire on your own terms. If that means quitting work at 55, that's fine. I've spoken with many people who never want to retire because they love their jobs. And heck, that's great too! Your goals are just that—yours.

This book is all about millionaire habits. Throughout these chapters, we will discuss what millionaire habits are, how they work, and ways you can use them in your life. The end of each chapter in Part 1 contains specific action steps for you to take to implement that chapter's habit. Don't skip that section. It's the most important part!

Best of all, you don't need to earn lots of money to make these habits work. All you need is the motivation and desire to become your family's first millionaire.

But I'll warn you right now: You can't be afraid of being selfish. Millionaires are selfish people, but not in the way you're probably thinking. Millionaires understand that nobody is responsible for providing for their families but themselves. And you need to understand that, too. It's okay to put yourself first. That's exactly what you should do.

If you're confused by how selfishness can be a good thing, don't worry. We talk about healthy selfishness and why it's a key component of building huge amounts of wealth later in Habit #2. For now, understand that selfishness is key to building a financially secure future for you and your family.

We Retired in Our 30s in an Airstream RV

Our story is a bit. . .unique. From the moment I set foot in an office for the first time, I knew this "working full-time" stuff wasn't for me. I didn't have everything figured out yet (far from it!), but I knew a 45-year career wasn't for me.

Throughout this book, I'll discuss details about how we managed to retire in our 30s. For now, just understand that my wife and I sold our homes, bought an Airstream RV, and set sail around the country full-time. For three years, that 200 sq ft trailer was our only home. And if that sounds small, that's because it was. Now add two dogs, and you have a good idea of how our post-work lifestyle went.

At least for three years.

It was fun as hell. We saw so many amazing areas of the United States. We spent our days hiking through forests, seeing national parks (ever been to Utah?), and adventuring to different wineries and breweries. It was a lot of fun, but after three years, we were ready to settle down onto our own little plot of land.

In 2019 we bought seven acres of land in the southern Arizona desert. Our home is completely off-grid. I affectionately dubbed our home the "off-grid recession-proof house", an accurate phrase considering the economy in 2023!

That's enough about me for now. Let's get into how this book is going to change your life so you can follow your dreams like we did, whatever they are.

How To Use This Book

This book is divided into two parts. I highly suggest you read them in order.

Part 1 discusses each of the ten millionaire habits and the millionaire wealth-building timeline. These habits are the building blocks for everything you do inside and outside your workplace. Millionaires use these habits to build money-making careers and live a life that's so satisfying that they can't wait to get up in the morning and start their day.

Part 2 dives into FIRE, or Financial Independence Retire Early. Younger people use these millionaire habits to work hard for several years and then quit their jobs in their 30s or 40s (hint: this was us). FIRE won't be for everyone, but its tactics can still make you very, very rich throughout your life. If you don't want to retire early, that's okay! But don't skip this part of the book. Achieving financial freedom is still the goal, and you might be surprised at the lifestyle options that open up to you once you're there.

If you are ready to put your old habits aside and start doing the things that attract wealth without thinking about it, continue reading.

You're in the right place.

Part 1

The 10 Habits of Millionaires
The Wealth-building Time Line

Like Rome, wealth wasn't built in a day.

Before diving into the nuts and bolts of millionaire habits, let's discuss the process virtually everyone goes through to build wealth. All millionaires go through this exact process, including me. The speed at which we go through each stage can differ from person to person, but it's almost impossible to skip any of these basic steps.

Sadly, some people work their entire lives and never get to the last stage, but this book will ensure you aren't one of those people.

I like to call this process the Wealth-building Time Line. It begins with earning income through jobs and side hustles and ends with reaching financial freedom, which means no longer having to work a day for the rest of your life (though you might still choose to).

Imagine getting up each morning without the horrifying beep of an alarm clock and deciding what to do with your day *right then and there*. This is what achieving financial freedom is all about. It gives you options. You can take full control of your life.

For some of us, this process might take several decades. For others, maybe just four or five years. But with few exceptions, this is the accumulation process we all go through.

The six-step wealth-building time line looks like this:

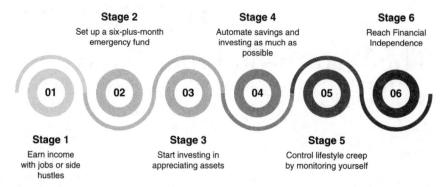

Stage 2
Set up a six-plus-month emergency fund

Stage 4
Automate savings and investing as much as possible

Stage 6
Reach Financial Independence

01   02   03   04   05   06

Stage 1
Earn income with jobs or side hustles

Stage 3
Start investing in appreciating assets

Stage 5
Control lifestyle creep by monitoring yourself

Let's discuss what happens in each stage of the time line.

Stage 1: Earn income with jobs and side hustles. This is where the magic begins. The accumulation of wealth begins with earning an income. Building wealth without earning an income is impossible unless you're the fortunate beneficiary of a large inheritance (this is rarer than many people believe). The larger the income, the more growth potential (but also the easier it becomes to spend money, which we will discuss later in this book).

Most of us will earn our income by working a full-time job. However, starting a business while working full-time (often called a "side hustle") can accelerate our income accumulation. For instance, you might design websites, walk dogs, or offer weekend landscaping services to make a little extra money. Interested? Ideas to maximize your income are in Habit #3. Every dollar you earn gets you one step closer to financial independence, regardless of where it comes from.

While earning a big salary is great, you don't need six figures to achieve financial freedom. Bigger salaries only shorten the time it takes to reach Stage 6.

Never forget that this is a process, not a race.

Stage 2: A three- to six-month emergency fund. Putting a little money aside for unexpected expenses is your emergency fund, and it should come before investing—and definitely before spending on nonessential items.

An emergency fund of at least three months of living expenses means you can endure most financial emergencies, sudden job losses, a leaky roof, or anything else that requires cash. While most financial "experts" recommend three months, I like six months to be extra safe. Whether you choose three months or six months will come down to your risk tolerance and whether you are a dual-income household. We will discuss how much to save in your emergency fund in more detail in Habit #7.

Your living expenses include everything that you spend money on month-to-month, including

- Rent or mortgage payments;
- Utilities (electricity, water, etc.);
- Food and groceries;
- Insurance (health, car);
- Cell phone bills;
- Household maintenance items such as cleaners.

Everything you spend during the month is a part of your living expenses.

For instance, if you spend $5,000 a month, saving three to six months' worth of living expenses adds up to $15,000 to $30,000.

"But Steve," you might say, "that's a lot of money to save! I don't have anywhere near that!"

That's okay. Three to six months is the goal, which takes time to reach. Later in this book, I will teach you exactly how to build your first emergency fund (or, if you already have one, to expand it) using automated techniques that will make this super easy. Believe me, it's much simpler than you probably think.

We will talk more about emergency funds and how to set your first one up in Habit #7.

Stage 3: Invest in appreciating assets. Nobody ever got rich by saving money alone. Instead, investments are what build wealth. There is always risk associated with investments, but investing in appreciating assets over the long term is how most people build enough wealth to achieve financial freedom.

Examples of long-term investing include:

- Stocks;
- Traditional 401(k)s and Roth IRAs;
- Real estate (properties and homes);
- Index funds, mutual funds, and ETFs;
- Gold, silver, and other precious metals;
- Collectibles such as art, antiques, and rare coins.

The stock market is one of the most common tools that millionaires use to build wealth over time. Most millionaires devote a portion of every paycheck to investing in the stock market, and many are rewarded with consistent growth over the course of 20, 30, or more years. This is called dollar-cost averaging. More on this in Habit #6.

Stage 4: Automate savings and investing as much as possible. Automation is the secret that millionaires use to take the discipline and guesswork out of accumulating wealth. It's the difference between humans tightening every screw on a new car and an assembly line of machines doing it instead. It's easy, repeatable, and consistent.

Automation refers to using computing routines to take action on our behalf at set intervals. Once we set these routines up, they work on their own without our involvement. We don't have to lift a finger! Automation helps us make Stages 1 through 3 easier because we no longer have to remember to save, invest, and transfer money between bank accounts. It just happens.

A few examples of automation include:

- Your employer's payroll system that automatically contributes a percentage of your paycheck to your 401(k) or Roth IRA;
- Bill pay systems that pay relatively consistent monthly bills such as your cell phone, television, streaming services, and utilities;
- Budgeting apps that help you save by transferring money from your checking account to a separate savings account every month.

I will show you how easy financial automation is to set up in Habit #6.

Stage 5: Control lifestyle creep. This stage sounds simple, but it's one of the most difficult steps for many people. Lifestyle creep happens when we inflate our lifestyle by spending more money as we earn more. It's also called lifestyle inflation, which plagues so many people. I was guilty of lifestyle creep when I was in my 20s, big time.

Here's the problem: when our lifestyle inflates alongside our income, we make it more difficult to build wealth because we keep spending more money. As I like to say, it's impossible to outearn bad spending habits.

Sure, we see high-income earners driving around in fancy cars, living in big homes, and wearing expensive jewelry and suits, but that doesn't tell the whole story. So many of these "millionaires" are actually in debt. Even with a high income, they've chosen to spend so much money that they aren't building wealth.

And here is why this stage is more difficult than it may sound. We work hard for our money. When that much-deserved raise finally comes around, we want to reward ourselves by spending a little of it to celebrate. All that overtime should count for something, right? After all, it's no fun to just save and not enjoy all that extra cash, right?

Actually, that's right. It is no fun.

This stage isn't about sacrificing your happiness by penny-pinching. It is okay to spend money to reward yourself for working hard and being successful. However, it's not okay to turn those celebration expenses into a regular part of your lifestyle—if you want to become a millionaire, that is. Spending all of your raises won't get you rich.

It will, however, increase the stuff you have lying around your house.

Controlling your expenses is an uncomfortable part of building wealth that many millionaires don't discuss. But I will show you exactly how to balance your life so you and your family can enjoy yourselves and build wealth simultaneously in Habit #9.

Stage 6: Financial independence. Congrats, you're there! This is what you've been working so hard to achieve. You're finally at the point where you have accumulated enough wealth to never have to work again, though you may still choose to work.

But don't be deceived! Never let your guard down. It's possible to lose financial independence if our spending gets too extravagant.

How do you know when you've reached financial independence?

I discuss the simple formula many millionaires use to calculate when they've reached financial independence (or how much they need to achieve it) in Part 2 of this book. The math is simpler than you probably think.

The wealth-building equation controls our journey to a million. The better you understand it, the faster the journey will be.

For the rest of Part 1, we will dive into 10 millionaire habits that will help you breeze through each phase of this process as quickly as possible, without sacrificing the things that make you happy.

Are you ready?

Habit #1
Millionaires Say Yes

Spend 10 percent of your time in your comfort zone and 90 percent of your time expanding it

I was 30 years old when I was called into the executive director's office.

My curiosity started spinning the moment I got the call. I'm a software engineer, so why does the executive director, whom we'll call Ben, want to talk to me? Ben was a very successful guy, wore expensive suits to the office, made lots of money, and had a big corner office. And I had never met with him before. What's going on?

"This can't be good," I told myself.

Worse, the meeting was on a Friday, and I had read somewhere that Fridays are common days to fire people. Walking into the meeting, I feared the worst. And I didn't feel any better after I noticed who else was there.

It was human resources! Why else would HR be in the room if I wasn't getting canned?

I took a seat and anxiously waited, fears racing through my mind. The instant Ben started talking, I braced myself.

Then, I relaxed.

"You're not getting fired," he said, sensing my concern. "In fact, it's the opposite."

It turns out the organization eliminated an entire layer of management above me, including the director of Information Technology, the director of System Operations, and the chief information officer. In one day, boom! They were gone.

That whole morning, the entire information technology department was operating without a leadership team and didn't even know it.

"We want you to take over as the Information Technology Department director," Ben said. "You've done good work, and we're confident you will excel in this position."

Wow.

I had thought about this day a lot. The day I finally got to be the boss and make lots of money. I wanted it so bad that I could taste it. And here it was. It was finally happening.

But there was a problem with what was happening. One minor detail.

I had no leadership experience! I had never been the boss at any place I worked. I didn't know how to lead. I was a software engineer that just turned 30. What did I know about leadership? And how could I possibly go from sitting quietly in my cubicle writing computer code all day to the corner office and managing people nearly twice my age?

It's not like this was a gentle step up. I wasn't becoming a supervisor or a shift lead. No, they wanted me to take the primary managerial role over the entire information technology department! This was not exactly the next step I had in mind. Becoming a supervisor was next, not the director.

I wanted to say thanks, but no thanks. I was not ready to leap up two layers of management in a single day, especially without any leadership experience to lean on. I was going to make a fool out of myself, I knew it. How could I go from working with my coworkers to suddenly being everyone's boss?

"Yes, let's do it," I replied.

Wait, what did I just say? "Are you crazy?" I mentally asked myself. Did I commit to getting in over my head, wearing suits to director's meetings, managing multimillion-dollar budgets, conducting performance reviews, and resolving employee conflicts— all without a shred of real-world experience?

Yep, that's exactly what I did.

Little did I know, getting an opportunity to jump multiple layers of management to a position of leadership that I wasn't ready for was my first exposure to how powerful millionaire habits can be. This was a test. It was like the world was telling me to either take advantage of this incredible opportunity or wait until it was too late.

I got a very rare opportunity to elevate my career. Even though I didn't feel ready, deep down I knew that I had to say yes. "I'll just figure it out as I go," I told myself. And that's exactly what I did. I made mistakes. But I learned on the fly. And, that Friday was the moment I drastically changed the entire course of my career.

And that brings us to our first millionaire habit. Millionaires say yes.

Do millionaires say yes to everything? Well, no. But consider this: often, it takes someone else's perspective to show us what we are capable of. We may not see it in ourselves, but someone else might. Another person represents an objective third party, and their endorsement means something special.

My organization would never have asked me to lead the Information Technology Department if they didn't think I could handle the responsibility. Their implicit confidence in my ability to do the job drove me to accept the big promotion.

That promotion changed my career prospects. In one day, I transitioned out of a technical career track and into a leadership track. And that transition came with exposure to a whole new world that taught me unique skills, connected me with higher-profile people, and boosted my salary for the rest of my career.

In one week, I went from earning $60,000 yearly to over $85,000. Back in 2012, this was respectable money for a 30-year-old.

Though a leadership role may not be right for everyone, think deeper about what this decision meant to my earnings potential throughout my career. Saying yes to this promotion put me on a different salary trajectory. A higher one.

Most cost-of-living raises are based on percentage. The higher your salary, the more additional money you will see in your paycheck.

For instance, a 5% raise on a $60,000 salary equals $3,000. After getting the raise, your new yearly salary is $63,000.

But, a 5% raise on an $85,000 salary is $4,250. This raise brings your yearly salary just shy of $90,000. A bigger raise due to the bigger salary.

Bigger salaries result in an exponential increase in earned income.

Consider the following table that illustrates these two salary trajectories over time. Notice how much faster the $85,000 salary grows compared to the $60,000.

$60,000 salary growth		$85,000 salary growth	
Annual raise %	Salary	Annual raise %	Salary
5%	$63,000	5%	$89,250
6%	$66,780	6%	$94,605
7%	$71,454	7%	$101,227
8%	$77,170	8%	$109,325
9%	$84,115	9%	$119,165

There is a substantial difference in these two salaries over a short five-year period.

Originally, there was a $25,000 difference between the $60,000 and $85,000 salaries. But after just five years, the salary difference jumped *another* $10,000.

This is the magic of exponential growth and why my decision to say yes impacted my income significantly. And this assumes that you didn't switch companies in those five years, which often results in an *even bigger raise.*

There are four reasons why saying yes more often will help you become a millionaire.

Reason 1: Saying yes helps you overcome your fears and insecurities, handle stress and rejection, and break out of your comfort zone so it doesn't hold you back. It creates an environment that embraces rejection and failure as part of the process rather than a roadblock that inhibits success. It healthily retrains your brain to jump in head first, learn as you go, and take the world by storm.

Saying yes is more than just a decision. It's a mindset built on positivity and confidence.

Reason 2: Saying yes makes you smarter. Everything you do—whether you succeed or fail, makes you smarter. New experiences help you learn about yourself and develop new interests. Experience = wisdom.

The more you say yes, the more exposure you have to new things. New ways of doing business. Saying yes will help you develop lucrative new skills that will make you more money in the future because you keep moving forward, putting yourself out there, and trying new things. The promotion I got taught me valuable leadership skills that helped me throughout the rest of my career.

We don't learn when we're living in our comfort zone. We only learn when we're out there in the real world and challenging ourselves.

Reason 3: Saying yes will instantly expand your personal and professional network. I believe in the phrase "It's not what you know; it's who you know." After my second job in the workforce, every other job came as a referral directly from someone inside my professional network (companies love it when employees refer candidates for job openings). The more you say yes, the more people you will meet.

The bigger your network, the more opportunities you will get. I always like to meet with at least one person from inside my network of friends and professionals at least once a month. Making an effort to regularly keep in touch opens the lines of communication in case I need to use them in the future.

Reason 4: Saying yes makes life more fun to live. Every time I said yes, I had a lot of fun. Sure, it was difficult at times during the learning process, but every opportunity I said yes to taught me something valuable that I took to the next opportunity.

Eventually, I started getting good at this stuff. I managed stress better. I recognized problems before they happened. I also knew that I could say yes to nearly anything and figure it out as I go. Let's face it: success is fun.

Three Ways to Say Yes

Saying yes to growth opportunities is not always as cut and dry as my promotion. Opportunities come in all shapes and sizes, and you might be surprised at how many of these opportunities you're already getting.

For example:

1. **Say yes to lunch with a colleague.** Grabbing lunch is a great way to chat about making money, discuss problems, or get to know the other person better. Improving relationships with friends and coworkers is a fantastic way to get new opportunities.
2. **Volunteer for that big project at work.** Pushing yourself outside your comfort zone helps you develop new skills and meet new people. And it might even teach you that you are more capable than you thought!
3. **Start that side hustle with a friend.** A side hustle is a small business you run during nights and weekends. Does your friend have a business idea about walking dogs using robots? Hear them out and, if it makes sense, build that robot to walk Rufus.

Am I Suggesting That You Say Yes to Every Opportunity You Get?

Certainly not. Saying yes to *everything* may not be in your best interest, and this would be extremely poor advice for me to give you.

For instance, saying yes to a new opportunity that would create an unhealthy work-life balance probably isn't the right choice. And clearly, it is not a good idea to get involved in so many different things that you burn out.

Nobody ever built meaningful wealth by working themselves ragged. That might work for a few months or even years, but eventually, the burnout will catch up with us.

Furthermore, I am a big believer in following your hunch. If your gut is telling you to say no, you might be wise to let that feeling guide your decision. My hunch has rarely steered me wrong!

Lastly, saying yes to an opportunity won't guarantee your success. In other words, saying yes won't necessarily mean it will work out. Sometimes you'll fail, and you need to be okay with that possibility.

After all, not all 30-year-olds get the chance to successfully lead a 40-person team of software developers every day. But even if an opportunity doesn't work out, we still learn valuable lessons to take to the next opportunity.

Embrace the power of yes, and watch your life transform.

Your challenge: Say yes to something new this week. Make it something you wouldn't have said yes to before reading this book. Just try it. It's okay if it's small. In fact, starting small is a good idea. For instance, ask a colleague you want to know better for lunch.

Take Action: Here's How to Say Yes More Often

Step 1: Identify areas in your life where opportunities exist. Give this step some time. It took me several weeks to realize how many opportunities I was getting (but ignored because it was easier to just say no).

For instance, I would routinely say no to projects I thought were "too hard," but those were often the opportunities that built the most skills and exposure. Unless something was both easy and exactly right, I'd say no. That was a mistake.

These opportunities may come from work, friends, family, classmates, etc. Remember that email you got two weeks ago from a colleague who wanted to have lunch? Or that job opening at work that you chose not to apply for? Or that chance to deliver an important presentation in front of your whole company?

These are all opportunities for you to prove yourself.

Step 2: Answer the question: Could I say yes? If so, what's stopping me from saying yes? Is it fear? Or is the opportunity truly not right for me? I don't want you to judge yourself during this step. Answer honestly.

In my case, I said no because I was afraid. I was afraid of failure or of making myself look stupid. But that was the wrong attitude. I was missing out on innumerable ways to improve my expertise and meet very successful people.

Step 3: Say yes unless your gut tells you no. If you already said no, reach out and change your mind. It's okay.

Devote an entire year to saying yes. It is okay if some opportunities don't work out. The point is to start putting yourself out there, challenging your comfort zone, and pushing through those self-imposed limits we all place on ourselves.

Habit #2
Millionaires Are Selfish

Our ability to give back and help others is immensely connected with our personal foundation

Most millionaires are selfish.

Not selfish in the traditional sense of the word. To use an airline analogy, millionaires believe in putting their oxygen masks on first before helping the person sitting next to them. The reasoning is brilliant: you can't help anyone if you're dead.

When your oxygen mask is on, your lungs have everything they need to keep your heart pounding and brain alert. As a result, you're in a position of strength. So when I say that millionaires are selfish, I'm talking about this. Millionaires are successful because they focus on self-care and their families first and their careers, entertainment, and social obligations second.

I am convinced that prioritizing your needs and building a strong and solid foundation for your life is one of the healthiest (and wisest) pursuits anyone can take.

Before I go any further, let me address the elephant in the room. Yes, there are exceptions to this rule. Some millionaires are selfish in an unhealthy way. They lie, cheat, and steal to get what they want. And when this happens, we often hear about it on the news. Or from friends and family lamenting an unfair corporate policy at work.

When a millionaire does commit a crime or gets caught doing unsavory things to make more money, we are quick to hear about it. The news loves plastering stories about the "evil rich" on television, saturating our minds with the inaccurate idea that most rich people are immoral, conniving, and selfish. But that couldn't be further from the truth.

As of 2022, there were almost 22,000,000 millionaires in the United States. If most of those 22 million people were evil, our world would look much different. Evil would ooze from every corner of society. It would be next to impossible for the rest of us to build wealth and provide for our families.

Luckily, most millionaires aren't evil.

Healthy Selfishness Means

Healthy selfishness is more than just caring for our basic needs. Yes, we need to address the necessities of life, such as keeping a roof over our heads and putting food on the dinner table every night. Those needs always come first.

Healthy selfishness takes the next step, allowing you to

- Enjoy a loving and supportive marriage or partnership;
- Feel comfortable at home and energized at the office;
- Maintain an emotional state free of worry and undue stress;

- Earn enough to not just provide the basics but also build wealth with enough left over to appreciate the finer things in life.

  When our minds aren't consumed by feelings of inadequacy and worry, they are free to seek out ways to give back and enjoy everything life has to offer.

How can you put healthy selfishness into practice? Relentlessly take care of yourself.

Let's talk about five key areas where taking care of yourself first will set you up to earn substantially more money, be happier, and put you in a better position to give back.

Finances

Money impacts every facet of your life. The car you drive, the home you live in, the clothes you wear, and the entertainment you enjoy are all influenced by money. The smarter you are with money, the stronger and happier you become, and the more you can spend on the things that are important to you.

Financial selfishness begins with understanding your personal goals and following five crucial financial strategies. Let's take a look at those strategies below.

Stay with me here. I promise this will all make perfect sense.

The Five Pillars of Financial Selfishness

Your financial health comes down to five key pillars:

- **Emergency fund:** Your emergency fund is money set aside for an unexpected expense such as a sudden job loss, car repairs, or a medical bill. Keep your emergency fund in a separate savings account to make it tougher to accidentally spend this money.

Aim for at least three months of living expenses, which include rent or mortgage, utilities, food, gas, travel, and entertainment.

- **Low consumer debt:** Not all debts are bad, but high-interest consumer debts are. High-interest consumer debts include credit cards, personal credit lines, and department store financing. Your goal is to keep consumer debt low (preferably nonexistent) and pay off the high-interest debt you already have.
- **Avoid living paycheck-to-paycheck:** Nothing is worse than being so strapped for cash that putting food on your dinner table *depends* on your next paycheck. Build enough of a buffer so you aren't dependent on your next payday to fund the necessities of life by keeping expenses low and maximizing your income. More on how to earn more money in Chapter 4.
- **Building wealth:** Building wealth is the result of saving, investing, and making smart financial decisions throughout your career. This requires earning more money than you spend, so there is enough left to invest in appreciating assets such as stocks, bonds, ETFs, and real estate.
- **Personal money goals:** Anything you're saving for, such as your child's education, a Caribbean cruise, moving to a warmer place after retirement, and so on.

If these five pillars aren't satisfied, you need to be more selfish with your money.

These pillars help us build enough wealth to retire comfortably on our terms. We cannot be so darn generous with our money that we weaken our financial future. Putting your financial health first will drastically improve your financial stability, giving you more resources to build your perfect lifestyle.

How can we be more financially selfish with our money? Consider this example.

Say you're out to dinner with a few friends. You're doing well at work, making good money, and feeling generous. The nice person you are, you decide to pick up the meal tab. The bill is $300, but who cares? You're doing well and have some extra cash to spend. You notice the waiter walking in your direction with the check and casually put your hand out, signaling you will take care of the bill.

Picking up the tab is nice, isn't it?

Sure, but it may not be the wisest decision depending on your overall financial health.

Is paying a $300 bill to be nice in your best interest?

There are several situations where forking over three Benjamins could put you in a worse financial position.

For example, if you have no emergency fund saved for an unexpected expense, you risk going into debt if you suddenly lose your job tomorrow or your roof springs a leak, requiring a costly repair. This isn't fun when you have money. It's less fun when you don't.

Or if you're in credit card debt, you're racking up an Mt. Everest-sized pile of interest (the average credit card interest rate is almost 22%!).[1] That credit card interest prevents you from achieving financial freedom, kills your credit score, and makes those credit card companies richer.

In other words, unless your financial position is solid (see the five pillars of financial selfishness), being nice could destroy your ability to save, build wealth, and retire on your terms as a millionaire.

Maybe that $300 could be better spent elsewhere. Or not spent at all.

You aren't required to pick up the bill at restaurants or give out loans to your friends and family, and this is especially true if you're racking up credit card debt, living paycheck-to-paycheck, not investing, or have no money saved for an emergency.

My advice: Your biggest priority is your own financial health, not "being nice" with your money. Remember that **you** are the only person responsible for paying your bills and building your dream life. Money is a huge part of that equation.

It's okay to be selfish with your money. Your financial well-being always comes first.

Health

There are two types of health, both important. And both types are equally dependent on each other. I am talking about your physical health and mental health.

Physical Health

Let's face it: We feel and perform better when in good shape. We are more energetic. Our sex lives improve. We also miss less work because regular exercise boosts our immune systems, putting us in a better position for promotions and raises.

It also means we spend less money on our health. *The New York Times* reported that people who exercise regularly before (or during) middle age save between $824 and $1,874 *each year* after retirement.[2] In addition, physical activity has been commonly shown to prevent obesity, diabetes, depression, and dementia. Not only will improving your physical health make you look and perform better, but it will also keep more hard-earned greenbacks in your pocketbook.

There's no downside to improving your physical health. The stronger we are, the more effective we will be in whatever we choose to pursue. In addition, healthy people are more energetic and creative, and keeping yourself in tip-top shape is one of the best ways to give back effectively.

As a result, your gym workout, yoga session, Zumba class, or run comes before anything else. Say no to distractions until your workout is done.

How can we start prioritizing physical health?

Step 1: It won't happen overnight. Don't expect miracles with this. Making major life changes—yes, even *healthy* life changes—take time. After all, we didn't put on an extra 30 or 40 pounds overnight, and it certainly won't come off that quickly either. Pace yourself and follow the process. Give it time.

Step 2: Use a schedule to make it a habit. Instead of trying to "fit in" time at the gym or to jog in nature, schedule that time. Make it a priority. Your schedule will help you turn your new fitness routine into a habit, not just something you do if you have time.

Are you a morning person? Try working out for 30 to 45 minutes before work. If you don't have time in the morning, try after work. For several years, I used to squeeze in a workout during my lunch break at a nearby gym, giving me a jolt of energy to push through the rest of the afternoon. I would eat lunch at my desk after the workout.

The important element to remember is to schedule your workout. If we decide to work out "if we have time," we probably won't make it most days because something will come up.

Step 3: Eat healthier. Eating healthier meals with vegetables and other whole foods improves your physical health. Dark green vegetables such as spinach, brussel sprouts, and broccoli are healthy green options. Other foods include whole grains such as quinoa and oatmeal, fish, berries, nuts, and seeds. Want a healthy snack? Try greek yogurt, frozen fruit, and hummus.

If you don't have time to shop for healthy foods, consider one of the many food delivery services such as Hello Fresh, Blue Apron, and Sunbasket. Pick your favorite meals and have all the ingredients shipped straight to your doorstep, complete with cooking instructions. Some even have ready-to-eat meals, making eating healthier foods at home just as convenient as picking up fast food on your way home from work.

Step 4: Find an accountability partner. Making big changes is hard for most of us, but finding someone to keep you accountable can be a game-changer. Just started a new workout program? Find a gym partner to work out with. Accountability partners will help motivate you to work out even if you're not in the mood.

Another good option is to use a mobile app to keep you motivated. MyFitnessPal, 8fit, and FitBod are three good options, but plenty of fitness apps can be installed on your phone to track your progress and remind you to get your workout in for the day. Apple iPhones can use the free "Fitness" app to track activities and set movement goals. Android users can use the "Google Fit" app to track calories, earn points based on activity, and track steps daily.

Step 5: Don't let a lack of time get in your way. If you can't make it to the gym, there are still plenty of ways to improve your physical fitness without it. For instance, park further away from the grocery store to help you get more steps. Take the stairs instead of the elevator. Use your lunch hour to walk around your neighborhood or office building. If you have the work flexibility, get an adjustable desk so you can stand up for portions of the day. Standing periodically helps your posture, and it burns more calories!

In addition, getting proper sleep is critical to increasing your energy, improving your mood, and boosting your mental health.

Pro tip: staying up super late on the weekends can worsen your Monday morning productivity. It can happen because drastically altering our sleep schedule messes up our circadian rhythm. Circadian rhythm refers to our natural physical and mental changes during a 24-hour period. The more consistent we are with sleep, the easier it becomes to wake up every morning ready to tackle the day.

For instance, I wake up naturally when the sun comes up. And likewise, I get tired shortly after dark each day. I learned the hard way not to fight it and say no to late-night invitations when I know it will ruin my morning the next day.

Mental Health

Research has shown that people who exercise regularly have better mental and emotional well-being and lower rates of mental illness.[3]

One of the biggest negative draws on our mental health is politics.

This might be a controversial statement, but I'm going to say it anyway: I am convinced that if people focused more on themselves and their own personal circumstances rather than consuming themselves with the latest political outrage, they'd be much happier, richer, and more content with the things they have.

What does this mean? It doesn't mean fighting for change or getting involved in the political system isn't valuable. History has clearly shown that governments only improve when the people stand up and fight for the changes they want.

But *consuming yourself* with politics can be a very unhealthy habit.

Here's the problem:

We humans have a way of focusing on distractions when something is fundamentally wrong in our lives. Focusing on those other things—be it politics, a cause, a social issue, or anything else—it is easy to neglect self-care. We become overly stressed. Angry. As a result, our performance at work might suffer. Our relationships get taxed.

Again—and I cannot stress this enough—this does not mean social issues and political causes are unimportant. Instead, it means when we look for things to fight against, we sometimes do so because we're dealing with a nagging problem in our lives.

And then we spend more time fighting than we do improving ourselves.

And here is the magic of healthy selfishness. When we focus on our needs before spending every waking moment consumed by politics or solving decades-long social problems, we better position ourselves to be effective agents of change because we're stronger and more confident people, free of undue stress and worry and ready to make profound differences in our communities.

We are only as effective as our minds and bodies allow us to be.

Bottom line: It's great to get involved in politics, social causes, and any other issue that's important to you. Just make darn sure not to neglect yourself in the process.

If you need help improving your mental health, the best thing to do is ask for it. Talk to someone you trust about what's going on in your life. Or call a crisis hotline for free help. Not ready to talk to someone over the phone? Check out crisistextline.org if you would rather text instead of talk.

Work

If you work 40 hours a week, that adds up to over 2,000 hours a year spent working. That's a heck of a lot of hours at the office. Our work also has a profound effect on our mood and mental health. If we feel like we are underpaid, it weighs on us. If we don't like our coworkers, we feel anxious and frustrated. Work is no place to let things get out of control.

If we aren't careful, work has a way of draining the life right out of us if we let it.

I'm here to teach you how not to let that happen.

We can boil down healthy selfishness at work into three main areas: compensation, work-life balance, and recognition.

Compensation

You are not being selfish or greedy by asking for a raise. In fact, it's the opposite.

Companies can let unfair or inappropriate compensation go unaddressed unless you are as proactive as possible in getting what you deserve.

First, make sure that you truly are underpaid. About twice a year throughout my career, I would use job posting websites such as Glassdoor and PayScale to find up-to-date salary information for similar jobs and companies. If I was underpaid, I made a note to talk to my boss about a compensation adjustment.

Be sure to consider any additional responsibilities above and beyond the job you were hired to do. For instance, I was hired as a software developer at my first employer but ended up managing their new intern program, where we hired and trained young students from a local university. This was clearly above and beyond what I was hired to do, and I used this extra responsibility to get an additional boost in my salary.

Pro tip: Look at your employer's own job postings for similar job roles. If their job description lists a salary higher than yours, that's a good indication that you probably need an adjustment in your salary. I used this technique at one of my former employers and instantly got a 4 percent raise to bring my salary in line with their job posting.

You might be underpaid at work if:

- You haven't had a cost of living adjustment in a year;
- Your responsibilities increased without a bump in your salary;

- You earned a certification or degree, making you more valuable;
- A friend tells you they make more money than you at another employer.

If you are underpaid, the next step is to talk to your boss about a raise. But before doing that, be sure to have supporting documentation that you are, in fact, underpaid.

Asking for more money can be challenging and stressful. However, it's an essential part of making sure you are paid what you are worth at work.

I go into exactly how to ask for a raise in Habit #3.

Work-Life Balance

Maintaining a healthy boundary between your work and home life doesn't mean you aren't committed to the job or don't care. It means you're prioritizing yourself and your well-being. And that will set you up for great things. Every time.

For a period in my life, my work-life balance was way off. I was always working. I remember doing work and sending emails on Christmas Eve. Checking in on Thanksgiving and vacation wasn't just common but expected. Just like overtime.

Saturdays and Sundays were a part of the workweek, and nobody seemed to question it (including me!). I always felt on the clock, whether or not I was. It wasn't until I gained about 75 pounds of fat and found myself out of breath after climbing a single flight of stairs that I realized I was slowly killing myself.

I was putting my job in front of everything, and that was a one-way street to nowhere.

I was working too much, and as a result, my health took a back seat. I never had the energy to cook, so I would grab something from a local restaurant or fast food joint on the way home. It destroyed my health and drained me of that hard-earned cash I was determined to make. My work-life balance was completely out of whack.

I needed to make a change. I knew my future happiness depended on it.

The change I made was a big one. I moved from Virginia to Arizona in search of a better work-life balance, and I found it. I was single then, so moving across the country was no big deal. I put in my two-week notice, packed my things, and drove west.

But let's face it: everyone can't just pack up and leave as I did. Many factors contribute to moving to another state when you're married with kids. Luckily, there are ways to take more control over your work-life balance without having to move.

Here are four ways to better manage your work-life balance.

1. Talk to your supervisor, manager, or human resources department to address your concerns. It's possible that they aren't aware of what's happening. Good companies want to ensure they aren't burning out their staff.

Here's what you might say in your meeting:

Over the past six months, I've put in over 50 hours of overtime and work most weekends, and it's beginning to have a negative impact on my energy. While I am willing to go above and beyond for the company, I also need to make sure my health and family life don't suffer. I would like to discuss ways to lighten my workload a bit so I can spend more time resting and with my family.

2. Set boundaries between your work life and home life. For instance, stop checking email after 6 p.m. on weekdays. Don't check your email at all over the weekend. Make it clear to your co-workers and boss that you step away from the computer after leaving the office and will reengage with work-related tasks the next business day.

3. Take more breaks. For many of us, just taking a few more breaks during the day can help us avoid being overwhelmed by work. In fact, one study found that taking a break from work increases focus and productivity when you return to work. It only takes a few minutes to reset your mind, process stress, and regain energy.[4]

If you work from home, stepping away from the computer might be easy. However, resist getting distracted by things at home (television, your kids, the laundry you forgot to take out of the drier, etc.).

If you work at an office, stroll to your breakroom for more coffee, tea, or water. On nice days, walk around the building a couple of times. Walking outside has the added benefit of temporarily changing your environment, which can drastically help you think through problems and develop creative solutions.

4. Switch jobs. If all else fails, don't be afraid to switch employers. Not only can this help you find a job with a better work-life balance, but changing jobs can also get you a higher salary. I switched jobs four times in about 15 years and got a 15–20 percent raise every time I took another position. You don't want to do this too much, but it can be an effective way to make more money and find a better position for you and your family.

Recognition

Valuing your contributions doesn't mean devaluing other people's work. If you worked hard on a project, hit a major milestone, or achieved something big, it's okay to raise your hand and take credit for what you did.

Let me tell you a short story about how important recognition can be.

In 2015, my company's chief operating officer (COO) asked me for help with a top-dollar proposal. It was for a big contract, and he wanted my input in writing some of the technical descriptions for the proposed work. Being the go-getter I was, I gladly accepted, thinking that this might "put my name on the map," as it were, at my company.

I mean, working directly with the COO is a great opportunity, right?

I spent a couple of days writing and then passed my edits to the contracts manager for review. A month later, my employer submitted the proposal to the customer. The contracts manager also sent me a copy of the proposal since I had a hand in it.

I won't leave you hanging—the company won the contract. But that's not why I am telling you this story. Let's go on.

Figuring this was a great time, I asked the COO for a raise. To help strengthen my request for more money, I mentioned the work I put into writing the winning proposal. Surely my help getting the company a multimillion-dollar deal was worth a little bump in my salary.

His response was something that I'll never forget:

I know you took a look at the proposal, but how much impact do you think you had on it? We weren't able to use a lot of what you wrote.

Wow, what a gut punch. I felt defeated. Even a little embarrassed.

Why would the COO ask for my help with the proposal if they didn't include any of my work? Maybe my writing wasn't good enough?

That afternoon, I was curious to see just how *little* of my writing they kept in the proposal, so I looked at the final document the contracts manager had sent me.

I started reading through the technical sections I had worked on, and my jaw dropped.

And my blood started to boil. Just a little bit.

Not only did my company use what I wrote, but they included a lot of my writing word-for-word. Entire paragraphs of technical details that I had written were kept in.

To be sure I wasn't crazy, I pulled up the edits I had sent a month ago. And yep, they included about 80% of what I wrote. Copy and paste. I had a huge impact on that winning proposal, but I wasn't getting any recognition for it.

So what gives? The COO told me they threw out most of my writing, but that wasn't true. My work was a big part of the proposal!

I wasn't sure how to feel. My initial reaction was pure anger. Was the COO messing with me? Was he unaware of how much of my work was kept in? Or maybe he was just being cheap and didn't want to give me a raise even though I deserved one?

At this point, I had an important emotional decision to make. I took the rest of the day to think about my next move. And I didn't want to make any hasty decisions I would regret later. I've been in that boat before, and it's not a fun boat to be in.

On one hand, I could have stayed upset and kept my mouth shut. Perhaps it just wasn't my time for that raise. Would raising a stink about it give me a bad name?

But on the other hand, I *had* written it, and my work helped the company get a lucrative contract due partly to what I wrote. Should I let this go or make an issue out of it?

I couldn't let it go. I had to say something.

In the most professional way I could, I told the COO that my writing *did* make it into the final contract almost word-for-word. I showed him the final proposal and the edits I had submitted a month ago. He had no choice but to recognize my impact in winning the contract, but only because I stood up for myself and chose not to let it slide.

I ended up getting the raise. And an apology to boot. It turns out the COO was unaware of how much of my work was kept. It was an honest mistake.

Not everything will work out as smoothly as this did, but standing up for yourself at work is a technique that millionaires use daily to ensure their contributions are recognized and paid accordingly. Getting recognized for your accomplishments isn't selfish. It's being proactive. And these recognitions can set you up for raises, promotions, and other opportunities because you prove your worth every day. Every accomplishment at work is like a step toward the finish line. You won't get to take that next step if you aren't recognized for your accomplishments.

Never forget: if you don't stand up for yourself, no one else will stand up for you, either.

Take Action: Here's How to Practice Healthy Selfishness

Step 1: Take care of your money. Nobody else is responsible for paying your bills and building wealth but you. Your financial health always comes before picking up the tab at a restaurant, loaning a friend some cash, or spending on frivolous stuff that will wind up in your closet in a month. The five pillars of financial selfishness position you to never worry about money again, and following these pillars is the best decision you will ever make.

Step 2: Take care of your body. Healthy people are more active, confident, and happy than those of us who let ourselves go and never exercise. It's okay to say no to that bar invitation if you want to reduce alcohol consumption. Or to say thanks but no thanks to staying out until 2 a.m. because it's the weekend. Take care of your body, and your body will take care of you.

Step 3: Take care of your mind. Your mental health profoundly affects your life, from the money you make to your happiness. If you need some quiet time, take it. If something feels wrong, say something. And if you need help, call someone to talk. Becoming a millionaire is easier for the mentally strong.

Step 4: Take care of your career. Stand up for yourself at work. If you deserve more money, ask for it. Talk to your boss or human resources if your work-life balance isn't working and you need to spend more time with your family. Don't stand by if you aren't being recognized for an accomplishment. After all, great opportunities only come around every so often. Exploit them when they do.

Notes

1. McCann A. "Average Credit Card Interest Rates." (August 2023). https://wallethub.com/edu/cc/average-credit-card-interest-rate/50841.

2. Reynolds, G. "Lifelong Exercise Adds Up to Big Health Care Savings." *The New York Times* (2021). https://www.nytimes.com/2021/06/16/well/move/exercise-health-care-cost-savings.html.

3. "Exercise and Mental Health." BetterHealth Channel (n.d.). https://www.betterhealth.vic.gov.au/health/healthyliving/exercise-and-mental-health.

4. "Take Back the Lunch Break." KRC Research (2017). https://cdntorkprod.blob.core.windows.net/docs-c5/763/185763/original/tork-takes-back-survey.pdf.

Habit #3

Millionaires
Maximize Income

I won't lie to you, making more money can be difficult. But it's also a critical component of achieving financial freedom, and it's something that nearly all millionaires know how to do quite well.

Why is increasing your income so important to becoming a millionaire? It's because inflation eats away at the spending power of each dollar you earn.

Inflation occurs when the price of goods and services increases over time, reducing your money's spending power. Many factors affect the inflation rate, such as supply and demand and fiscal policies. Don't worry, I won't bore you with an in-depth discussion of inflation. The important thing to remember is inflation reduces the value of each dollar you earn, making it essential to keep your salary going up each year.

Take home values, for example.

The median home value in 2000 was $119,600. Today, it's north of $380,000 (and continuing to rise). Doing the math, buying the same home today costs more than three times as much as it did in 2000. This is the result of inflation at work.

The goal: **Make your salary go up every year at a *higher rate* than inflation.**

How high, you might ask? Between 1960 and 2021, the average inflation rate was 3.8% (with a total overall inflation rate of over 800%!). This means if you didn't keep your salary going up by at least 3.8%, you essentially got a pay cut because your spending power decreased. The price of goods and services went up faster than your raises.

I cannot stress enough how important it is to keep your income growing!

Here's a chart of the US Bureau of Labor Statistics inflation rate. Note the steep rise and fall of inflation. This chart helps prove that *deflation* is rare (where prices drop), and it's much more common for the price of goods and services to increase over the years.

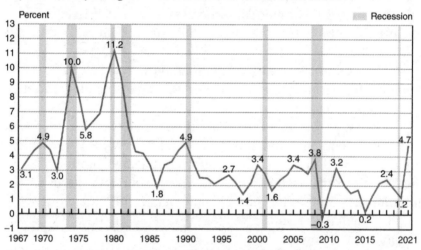

Annual Percent Change of the Consumer Price Index Retroactive Series (R-CPI-U-RS) Using Current Methods All Items: 1967 to 2021

Note: The U.S. Census Bureau uses the Bureau of Labor Statistics' (BLS) Consumer Price Index for all Urban Consumers Retroactive Series (R-CPI-U-RS) for 1978 through 2021. In 2021, BLS renamed the Research Series (CPI-U-RS) the Retroactive Series. For 1967 to 1977, the Census Bureau uses estimates provided by BLS from the CPI-U-X1 series. The CPI-U-X1 is an experimental series that preceded the CPI-U-RS and estimates the inflation rate in the CPI-U when applying the current rental equivalence method of measuring the cost of homeownership for years prior to 1983. More information on the R-CPI-U-RS is available at <www.bls.gov/cpi/research-series/r-cpi-u-re-home.htm>.

Source: U.S. Bureau of Labor Statistics

My salary reached the six-figure mark in my late 20s (when earning over $100,000 a year was considered a high salary). Earning a high salary gave me more money to save and invest, which helped me accumulate enough to quit corporate America in my 30s.

It wasn't because I was the best or the brightest in the company. In fact, my skills were fairly mediocre in many of the offices I worked.

I maximized my income because I did a few important things right over the course of my career. And these choices kept my income going up year after year.

Switch Companies

I kept my salary going up throughout my career by regularly switching companies.

Every three to four years, I looked for another job. In my line of work, changing jobs fairly often wasn't unusual. Fortunately, it also helped my salary continuously increase faster than it would have and *much faster* than the inflation rate.

According to one study, wage growth for those who switch jobs is almost 50% higher than for those who stay in their current jobs.[1] 50% higher! My experience matched that study's findings.

Traditionally, my employers gave cost-of-living wage increases of around 3% to 4% to keep up with inflation. In the years I switched companies, however, **I got anywhere from 10% to 15% raises**, typical for most job switchers. My salary easily outpaced inflation because the boost in salary was higher than the cost-of-living raises I would have received if I had stayed put at the same employer.

In other words, a 15% raise is a heck of a lot better than a 4% raise.

Does this mean you'll always get a 15% raise each time you switch jobs? Not necessarily. But the numbers also don't lie. On average, those who change jobs regularly throughout their career earn more money than those who stay in place.

"But Steve," you might ask, "isn't it possible to switch jobs too often?"

Yes, it is. The downside to changing jobs is if you do it too often, it can hurt your job prospects. If a future employer thinks you'll bail in a year or two, they might pass on your application. Employee turnover is very expensive.

When it comes to switching companies, carefully consider how much is too much. In information technology, changing jobs every three to four years is typical. But your industry might be different. It will also depend on your level of seniority (switching jobs is more common in lower levels of seniority than higher ones).

Before submitting your resume to other companies, ensure you're not hurting your chances of finding work by switching jobs too frequently.

Start a Side Hustle

A side hustle is a great way to boost your income without switching jobs or asking for a raise at work (or if you're properly motivated, *in addition to* asking for more money at work). Good side hustles can bring in anywhere from $500 to $5,000 a month of extra income. This extra money will make a big difference in your ability to save and invest.

As the name implies, a side hustle is a business you run on the side (in other words, nights and weekends). The idea is for that side hustle to generate additional income outside your regular nine-to-five job without taking up all of your free time.

A side hustle can provide additional income to help you keep up with inflation.

For example, let's say you have a full-time job that pays $80,000 annually, and inflation is running at 4% per year. After one year, your purchasing power will be reduced by 4%, which means you'll need to earn an additional $3,200 per year just to keep up with inflation (80,000 × 0.04). Starting a side hustle that generates an extra $3,200 annually (or more!) ensures that your purchasing power remains intact.

There's another great benefit of starting your own small business on the side.

A side hustle can provide a safety net in case you unexpectedly lose your full-time job. It's always a good idea to have a backup plan if things don't go as planned. A profitable side hustle provides an additional source of income to help you pay your bills and cover your expenses until you find another job.

Lastly, a side hustle can offer a sense of purpose and fulfillment outside of your nine-to-five job. Turning your hobbies into profitable small businesses allows you to pursue them more fully and potentially turn them into full-time businesses.

A deep discussion about starting your own business is beyond the scope of this book, but I would be remiss if I didn't give you a broad overview of the process that so many millionaires have taken to build their side hustle businesses.

Here's a six-step road map to starting your own business:

Step 1: Commit for at Least a Year

It's easy to quit, isn't it? Really, it's too easy.

Challenge yourself to commit to your small business for at least a year before giving up and trying something new. I've witnessed countless people give up after just a couple of months, and that's often too soon to tell whether your business idea will pan out.

Keep in mind that most side hustle businesses don't make money immediately. It can take some time before it becomes profitable. Giving up too soon means you won't give your business the time to turn the corner into a money-making venture.

Step 2: Identify Your Money-making Strengths

If you're struggling with what type of business to create, it's helpful to identify what you're good at first and then work backward from there.

For instance, if you enjoy working outside, perhaps a landscaping or yard maintenance company is up your alley (people pay

handsomely for someone else to mow and maintain their yards!).
You could even pull in $15 to $20 an hour just walking dogs
around your neighborhood. People spend a lot of money on their
pets, too.

Still not sure what side hustle business to start? Here are 20
quick ideas to get your creative juices flowing:

1. **Tutoring:** work with students who need help learning a topic you know about;
2. **Freelance writing:** write content for those needing blog posts, articles, marketing material, or other written content;
3. **Graphic design**: create logos, banners, and other visual content;
4. **Social media management:** manage social media accounts for businesses or individuals who don't have the time or expertise to do it themselves;
5. **Web development:** build websites for businesses who need an online presence;
6. **Dog walking or pet sitting:** care for those furry loved ones while their owners are away;
7. **House cleaning:** clean homes or office buildings for those who don't want to do it themselves;
8. **Personal shopping:** help people who don't have the time or can't shop find the clothes and accessories they need;
9. **Event planning:** plan parties, weddings, and other events;
10. **Language translation:** translate documents or help people communicate in different languages;
11. **Photography:** make photos for clients who need imagery for their websites or social media accounts;
12. **Podcast production:** help people create and edit their podcasts;
13. **Virtual assistant:** help busy professionals manage email, schedule, and other repetitive or common administrative tasks;
14. **Online coaching:** offer coaching services for people who want to improve their skills or achieve their goals;

15. **Personal training:** change people's lives by training them to get into shape or suggesting diet plans for weight loss;

16. **Food delivery:** shop and deliver groceries to people's homes and businesses;

17. **Lawn care:** mow lawns and offer yard maintenance services in your area;

18. **Handyman services:** offer your skills in plumbing, electrical work, or other handyman tasks to people who need help;

19. **Music lessons:** give music lessons for people who want to learn how to play an instrument;

20. **Car detailing:** clean and detail cars for people who want to keep their vehicles looking new.

Step 3: Validate Your Idea with Market Research

Before diving too deep into your business idea, make sure people are willing to pay you for your product or service by doing a little market research.

For example, let's assume you want to open a dog-walking business in your neighborhood. To validate your idea, ask yourself a few questions:

- Do people in my neighborhood have dogs?
- Are they willing to pay someone else to walk them?
- Does anyone else in my neighborhood offer these services?
- If so, how much do they charge? Can I do a better job and charge less?

If you're not sure about your competition, use Google and search for dog walking services in your area. Check out their pricing. What are their hours? Do they have good reviews? Do they appear to be successful at it?

Of course, the less competition you have, the better your chances of success. But don't be discouraged if you find others out there who walk dogs. Your goal is to differentiate your services from others, not find an idea that literally no one else is doing.

Perhaps you'll offer the same service for a cheaper price. Or maybe you will offer a better service for the same price.

There are plenty of ways to separate yourself from your competition. Remember that every business goes through this same process.

Step 4: Find Your First Paying Customer to Confirm Your Idea

After validating your idea as good, it's time to find your first paying customer.

You might have to ask around at first to get your first customer because you aren't yet known as the neighborhood dog walker. Ask your friends with pets if they want to regain some of their time by paying you to walk their dog. Put up a flier. Do whatever it takes to get your first paying customer.

It's tempting for some people to offer their services for free initially. Resist doing that! This step aims to find out if people are willing to pay you to provide your dog walking service. Don't give your service away for free!

After finding your first paying customer, confirm that your idea will work.

A few questions to consider:

- Do you like walking other people's dogs?
- Is this something you see yourself doing after work or on the weekends?
- Are people okay with paying the price you've set for your services?

If the answer to those questions is yes, you have your first side business idea!

If the answer is no, that's okay. Try another one by going through the same process until you find the perfect side hustle business for you.

Step 5: Build Your Business!

This is where your business really begins to take off. You've validated your idea. You even found your first paying customer and are convinced that your business idea is good. Now is your chance to go all-in.

When you go all-in, you've committed to the idea. You've told yourself, "I am determined to make this business work!" It's your time to shine.

Here's what you need to do:

- **Branding:** A logo, website, business card, and vanity email address (you@yourcompany.com) are all a part of your small business's brand. The branding step may not be critical for some businesses, but for others, it will be. You will at least want a business card or brochure to give to potential customers.
- **Find customers:** Finding more paying customers is the only way your business will take off. Use the branding material you've made to help. Give out your business cards to friends. Advertise online or in a local newspaper. Pay your friends a referral fee if they refer a paying customer to your business.
- **Develop a process:** What happens when someone wants your service? The entire start-to-finish customer process needs to look polished and professional; this step will take some trial and error. That's okay. The point is to develop one and stick to it. For instance, will you require a deposit before work begins? Will you check in with the customer halfway through a bigger project? After the work is done, will you ask for positive reviews or testimonials online?
- **Set milestones for success:** Establish short-term and long-term goals for your new side hustle. For example, maybe you want to make $250 a month by the end of the year. Or perhaps you want at least 30 customers by this time next year. Keep your milestones realistic and achievable. Expecting $10,000 a month right after starting isn't practical. But $250 a month might be.

Step 6: Check In Regularly

Make it a point to check in with yourself every so often to confirm the business is going well and you're still enjoying it. Include your spouse and family in the discussion if you can to make sure everyone gets their voice heard. When you first begin, check in every month. Then, check in every quarter. After, have your discussion at least once a year.

A few questions to answer during your check-ins include:

- Are my prices reasonable?
- Do I still want to run the business?
- Is the business taking too much of my time?
- Has it negatively affected my work-life balance?
- Am I bringing in enough income to justify my time?

Use these questions to adjust your business or the hours you work so the side hustle business makes the most sense for you and your family.

Ask for a Raise

Asking for more money at work is often the simplest way to boost your income. It's simple, but it's not always easy.

In fact, asking for a raise can be downright nerve-racking!

I remember counseling a coworker who was underpaid to ask for a raise. He was bitter about making less money than his peers but refused to ask for more money. When I asked him why, he said, "I can't do it because I don't want them to say no."

In truth, he wasn't just nervous about asking for more money. He was fixated on the possibility of getting the "no" and feeling embarrassed. He didn't want to be seen as a complainer or not a team player when in truth, all he did was hurt his career.

By not asking for more money, he set his career income potential back.

Remember the table of two salary trajectories from <u>Habit #1</u>? My coworker's refusal to ask to be fairly compensated kept him on a lower-paying salary path that, come retirement, will negatively affect his post-work lifestyle.

I cannot stress enough how important it is to get paid what you are worth. You are not being selfish (in a bad way) by asking for more money when you are underpaid. No, you're being proactive. Proactive people make substantially more money than those who just sit back and hope everything becomes fair. Unfortunately, it probably won't.

To be paid what you are worth, sometimes you need to ask for it. Here's how to ask for more money at work (and get it):

How to Ask for More Money at Work

Asking for a raise at work can be a nerve-racking experience. I remember how nervous I was the first time I asked for an adjustment to my compensation. I was sweating bullets and afraid my boss would say no or think less of me. But remember, good companies always pay their employees fairly because they know how valuable good workers are. They can't afford to lose them!

Here's how to ask the right way for a salary adjustment:

Step 1: Map out your accomplishments

Write down all of your major accomplishments and accolades. For instance:

- Did you deliver on a big project and exceeded expectations?
- Are you doing more work than you were hired to do?
- Did you receive a glowing customer review?
- Did you set a new sales record?

In other words, why do you deserve a raise? Make it easy for your employer to say yes by proving why you are a valuable asset to the company. Your accomplishments are proof. Take time to write these down.

Step 2: Decide what you want

Too many people ask for a raise and then get that deer-in-the-headlights look when their bosses ask, "How much do you want?" If you get this question, you need to have an answer ready, "I don't know" isn't a good answer. It means that you're unprepared and didn't do your homework. Know your number.

Not sure what to ask for? Remember, this is a negotiation. **It's wise to ask for a little more than you want.** This gives your employer a buffer to bring the raise amount down while still giving you what you want to get.

A number of factors will influence your number, including:

- Your current salary;
- How long you've worked *there*;
- How long you've worked *in your career*;
- Your performance reviews and accomplishments.

In general, I recommend asking for at least 10 to 15% more than you're making right now. For example, if you're making $75,000, you might ask for a $7,500 to $11,000 raise. This might seem like a lot, but remember you are giving your employer room to bring that number down. If you want a $5,000 raise, tell your boss that you're looking for $7,500. If they offer you less (say, $4,000 or $4,500), you're still close to the raise you wanted. If you only ask for a $5,000 raise, they may only give you $2,500 or less. Always ask for more than you want.

Step 3: Schedule a meeting with your boss

Understand that timing can be everything. For instance, you might jump the gun if you haven't had your first yearly performance review yet or have only worked for your employer for less than a year. Or if your employer is undergoing layoffs, it's probably not the right time.

In addition, always ask for a raise in person whenever possible. After all, it's an important conversation and deserves a face-to-face meeting (and it's easier to say no in email than it is in person!).

Send an email to your boss requesting a meeting to discuss your compensation. Try not to send this email when they are busy. Pick a time when things are slower to increase your chances that a meeting gets scheduled soon.

Your email might look something like this:

Hi Bob/Barbara,

I've been working extremely hard this year and would love to schedule a meeting with you to discuss my compensation to account for the extra work I'm putting in. Would you have time in your schedule to talk about this on Friday?

Step 4: Confidently deliver your request

Rehearse your argument, and bringing notes with you to the meeting is okay. Don't worry, you're not delivering a PowerPoint presentation here. You're just talking with your boss. It's a conversation.

Here is what you might say:

Thanks for meeting with me, I appreciate your time. I would like to discuss a compensation adjustment, given that I've taken on more responsibilities in my role, such as spearheading our new customer service initiatives and training our new hires on our software process. In addition, I've received exemplary remarks from our customers; many of them ask to talk to me when they call in with a problem because they trust me. Lastly, over the past six months, I've *put in over 50 hours of overtime to prepare our new soft-ware product. I am hopeful we can raise my salary by $X to account for my accomplishments.*

Here is another example:

I appreciate your meeting with me to discuss my salary. It's been more than a year since my last salary adjustment, and I've noticed that many similar roles in this area are paying $X more than I am making. My last performance review was excellent, and I constantly go above and beyond in my role. For example, I solved that big issue we were having with our scheduling software, saving Tim a lot of time in correcting scheduling problems with our customers. I've also taken on more responsibility in the last year, like coordinating meetings between our customers and us. I would like to discuss at least a 5% cost of living raise.

Understand that it might not be up to your boss to approve your raise request. He or she will likely need to send your request up the food chain before giving you a yes or no answer. If this happens, don't be discouraged. It's normal. However, make it a point to follow up in a week if you haven't heard back.

What about Investing?

You might be curious why I haven't mentioned investing in this chapter. There is a good reason for that. Investing is a great way to build wealth (in fact, it's essential). However, this chapter is about increasing your income through salaries and side hustles. But don't worry, we will chat in depth about investing, how to do it right, and ways to make it simple, later on in this book.

Take Action: Here's How to Maximize Your Income

Step 1: Survey the job market. Even if you have no interest in switching companies, it's always wise to stay up on industry trends and salaries for similar job roles as yours. If you don't plan to move, you can still use bigger salaries in job listings at other companies to increase your salary at your existing employer.

Step 2: Start a side hustle. Starting a business along with working a full-time job can be a great way to boost your income.

Step 3: Ask for a raise. If you think you are underpaid at work, don't hesitate to ask for more money. Reputable companies always want to pay their staff a fair salary. Do a little due diligence by researching similar jobs at other companies for comparable salaries. Remember that any additional responsibilities you've taken at work are also grounds for a compensation adjustment.

Note

1. Kolmer, C. "26 Average Salary Increase When Changing Job Statistics." Zippia (2023). https://www.zippia.com/advice/average-salary-increase-when-changing-jobs.

Habit #4

Millionaires Pay Themselves First

Do not save what is left after spending, but spend what is left after saving.

—*Warren Buffett*

If you hate budgeting, then let me introduce you to one of the best money-management techniques that doesn't require you to budget. You won't need to keep meticulous track of your spending, either.

Using the Pay Yourself First plan, you prioritize funding your savings and investment accounts before spending money anywhere else, making everything left over from your paycheck almost like free money that can be spent with zero guilt.

Before discussing how this works, let's talk about how most manage their money.

Most people spend first and then save and invest what's left over (maybe). In other words, they pay bills, make purchases, cover expenses first and then set aside whatever money is left over for savings or investments. This is the opposite of Pay Yourself First and requires significantly more discipline to build wealth. It drastically reduces the ability to save and invest because there may not be much left over after expenses are paid.

For the record, this is how I spent at least the first half of my adult life.

The second I got my paycheck, I looked for places to spend. Since photography was a hobby of mine, I would buy new cameras and lenses all the time.

Photo equipment isn't cheap!

Going out to eat wasn't just something I did on special occasions. No—as a highly paid software engineer who deserved the nicer things in life, I went out to eat almost every day throughout my early career.

And for a three-year period, I ate out for *every meal* (not exaggerating). Lunch and dinner every day. Not only was I packing on a bunch of additional weight, but I was spending insane amounts of money for the privilege of not cooking (but on the bright side, my roommate and I had the cleanest stove in the apartment complex because we had never used it in three years).

And don't think I didn't budget. I did.

Every month, I would put virtual dollars into spending categories up to my paycheck amount. If my paycheck was $2,000, for example, I would divvy up that $2,000 into different spending categories so I knew how much I could spend and on what.

And every month, I would steal from budget categories where I was spending a little less. If I didn't drive as much last month, I'd have a little extra money left in my gas category that I would steal to go out to eat or buy something that I wanted.

In the end, I wasn't getting wealthy. I didn't let my budget stop me from spending on what I wanted. But because I still had a budget, I didn't feel like I was doing anything wrong. I understand now that I was. I was stealing from my future self.

Eventually, I got wise about what I was doing to my future self.

I didn't know about the Pay Yourself First plan then, but I wish I did. It makes it virtually impossible to steal from yourself and cheat your budget because, technically, there isn't a budget at all. It's a beautiful system, which we will look at now.

How Does Pay Yourself First Work?

What if I told you that you could buy whatever you want with zero guilt without keeping a detailed record of your spending? Would you be interested?

That's exactly how Pay Yourself First works.

Pay Yourself First is a technique that prioritizes your savings and investing goals before spending on other expenses. The concept is based on the idea that by saving first, you ensure that your long-term financial goals are met and reduce the temptation to spend all your income on short-term—and in my case, usually stupid—desires.

Here's how the technique works:

Set financial goals: Saving becomes much easier when there is something that you're saving for. For instance, your goals might be paying off your home's mortgage, sending your kids to college, or taking that dream vacation to Fiji. Create a list of short-term and long-term financial goals and slap it on your refrigerator next to your daughter's awkwardly honest school drawing of you drinking wine like it's going out of style.

Be sure to put an estimated dollar figure next to each savings goal. If that Fiji vacation will cost $10,000, include that number.

Establish savings benchmarks: Once you have identified your financial goals, set a specific savings goal for each. This could be a percentage of your income, a fixed monthly amount, or a specific dollar amount. For instance, you might set aside $50 a paycheck for your trip to Fiji. Or maybe you are okay with putting 10% of your paycheck aside to pay for your child's future college education.

I like using separate savings or money-market accounts for my savings goals. Keeping this money separate makes it less likely to be accidentally spent.

Automate your savings: Use automated bank transfers to set money aside into a separate savings account every month. Again, physically separating your savings from your primary checking account (where your paycheck is deposited) makes it tougher to accidentally spend (or steal!) money you are trying to save. We talk much more about using the power of automation in <u>Habit #5</u>.

Automate your investing: If your employer offers traditional 401(k) or Roth IRA, use automatic payroll deductions to invest in your long-term retirement accounts. If you don't have access to employer-sponsored investment accounts, use automated bank transfers to fund a brokerage account or any other type of investment. We take a deep dive into investment options in <u>Habit #6</u>.

Keep yourself honest: After fully funding your savings and investing goals, the rest of the paycheck is yours to spend in any way you like. Resist stealing money from your savings or investments to make non-essential purchases like season tickets to a sports team, eating out, or taking pricey vacations. Pay yourself first will only work if your spending aligns with your financial goals and you stick to your spending plan.

Monitor your progress: Regularly review your savings and spending to ensure you're on track to meet your financial goals. Adjust your savings and spending as needed.

The Pay Yourself First technique can help individuals build wealth and achieve financial security over time. By prioritizing savings, you can reduce financial stress and have the peace of mind that you're working toward your long-term goals.

If you're a little unclear about how this works in practice, let's consider an example.

How Pay Yourself First Works

Here's an example of how the Pay Yourself First principle works.

Suppose you have a monthly take-home income (after taxes) of **$6,000**. You prioritize saving and investing before spending on discretionary items, the primary philosophy behind the Pay Yourself First plan.

This is how you might manage your money.

Step 1: Establish your goals. Your financial goals include building at least a three-month emergency fund, setting money aside for your child's college education, saving money for a downpayment on a future home, and investing for retirement.

To do this, you will **save**:

- $300 into your emergency fund;
- $1,000 for your child's college;
- $200 for a house down payment.

And you will **invest**:

- 20% of your income in a long-term retirement account, such as a traditional 401(k) or Roth IRA: $1,200;
- 10% of your income in an investment account of index funds: $600.

In total, you're setting aside $3,300 a month to fully fund your savings and investing goals.

Step 2: To make saving and investing easy, you use automated systems to transfer money into your separate savings accounts and investment funds every month. You set up automated bank transfers of $300 to your emergency fund account, $1,000 to a college savings account, $200 for your future down payment on a bigger home, and $600 into an investment account. You also use your employer's payroll system to deduct 20% of your paycheck into your long-term retirement account. If you aren't sure how to set up these automated systems, don't worry. Habit #5 discusses how to use the incredible power of automation in much more depth.

Step 3: Once your savings and investments are funded, you allocate the rest of your income toward your monthly expenses, such as rent, groceries, gas, and other bills. You spend $1,600 a month on your monthly bills.

Let's do some quick math. You're using $3,300 of each paycheck to save and invest. Another $2,100 is used for regular monthly expenses to keep the lights on, gas in the car, and food on the table.

Step 4: Lastly (and this is the fun part!), you can use any remaining money from your paycheck for discretionary spending, such as entertainment or dining out. Combined, you're using $5,400 a month of your paycheck to completely take care of your lifestyle, savings goals, and long-term investments.

That leaves $600 left over.

Here's the beauty of Pay Yourself First: This $600 is free money. You can use it for whatever you want, guilt-free. After all, you've already saved enough and fully funded your investment accounts. You've already paid your bills. Everything is taken care of. All that's left to do is enjoy what is left over.

Setting up Pay Yourself First for the first time will be an iterative process as first. For instance, you might discover that you don't have enough money left over to spend on everything that you're used to. This isn't necessarily a bad thing! After all, spending less money on non-essentials is a great way to build long-lasting wealth.

If you want more money to spend after your savings and investment goals are fully funded, then you have two options:

1. Make more money, which we discussed in Habit #3; or
2. Spend less money, which we will discuss in Habit #9.

I will be honest, part of this process will be uncomfortable. It will include deciding what spending is most important and what isn't. You will probably need to reduce your discretionary spending (spending on nonessential items) as part of this process, but that's not bad. Cutting spending is a natural part of the wealth-building process.

When Is Pay Yourself First Not a Good Idea?

I love this money-management technique because it's easy and takes the guesswork out of managing your money. It's also a technique millionaires use to build wealth and stay out of debt without a budget.

Pay Yourself First is even embraced by billionaire investor Warren Buffett, who once said, "Do not save what is left after spending, but spend what is left after saving."

However, that doesn't mean it will be right for everyone.

When is Pay Yourself First not a good idea? There are several circumstances where the Pay Yourself First plan may not be right for you.

1. You have high-interest debt: High-interest debts, such as unpaid credit card balances or payday loans, should always be prioritized before anything else, even investing. Interest charges on your debt will likely be higher than the potential returns on your savings, making it more financially sound to eliminate these debts first.

Even with debt, saving for a rainy day is still a good idea. However, it's wise to devote as much money as possible to paying off your credit card debt as soon as possible, as running a credit card balance incurs high-interest charges and hurts your credit score.

2. You have unexpected expenses: If you have an urgent and unexpected expense, such as a medical bill or a car repair, it may be necessary to prioritize paying for that expense instead of paying yourself first. Of course, having an emergency fund set aside specifically for these types of expenses is important, as your rainy day fund can prevent you from going into debt or putting your financial goals on hold.

Let's say your home's roof springs a leak, requiring a pricey fix. Maybe it costs $12,000 to repair. You might have used your credit card to pay for the fix. As a result, paying off that credit card should be your priority.

3. You have an unstable income: If your income is inconsistent, committing to a Pay Yourself First plan may be difficult. Focusing on budgeting and managing your expenses may be more appropriate until you have a more stable income. In addition, keeping a little extra money in your checking account might be wise to help fund living expenses during months with less income.

Take Action: Here's How to Get Started with Pay Yourself First

Step 1: Use systems. The Pay Yourself First plan will be much easier if you use automated systems to transfer money to where it needs to be. Once these systems are set up, you must continue earning a paycheck. Pay Yourself First still works if you don't have access to automated systems (or are unwilling to use them). It will just take a little more effort on your part.

For example, use your employer's payroll system to fund your long-term retirement accounts automatically. Then, use your bank's online system to set up monthly money transfers from your checking into your savings account (your emergency fund) and any other investment accounts you have. Remember to put enough money aside from every paycheck to meet your savings goals, such as a home down payment or your child's college.

In addition, use auto bill pay to make it easy to pay fixed monthly bills (streaming services, cell phone, mortgage/ rent, etc). Since these bills tend to be consistent, predicting spending in these areas should be easier.

Again, Habit #5 takes an in-depth look into using automation to make it much easier to manage your money.

Step 2: Spend without guilt. After you have saved, invested, and paid your bills, everything left over is free money. Spend it as you wish. Remember that if you spend some of this money on recurring monthly services (food delivery, another streaming service, memberships, etc), your regular monthly bills will increase, leaving you with less extra money in the future.

Habit #5

Millionaires Automate Everything

Have you ever heard the phrase "Set it and forget it?" It's exactly what happens when you start using automation to help you manage your money.

About 10 years ago, I got to the point in my life where I didn't have to do anything after getting my paycheck. Before the check hit my bank account, my employer's payroll system automatically put a fixed percentage into my 401(k), and Roth IRA accounts. The remaining amount was deposited into my checking account.

But the automation didn't stop there.

I set up monthly automated transfers from my checking account into a separate savings account to build up my emergency fund and meet short-term and long-term savings goals. This happened on the 15th of each month like clockwork. It took me about five minutes to initially set up, and it just worked without me thinking about it.

Also, I have never paid a single late fee or penalty in my life because I use automation to ensure all of my bills are paid in full and on time.

Whenever I could, I used auto bill pay to automatically pay my recurring monthly bills, such as my cell phone and cable television bill, homeowners association fees, car and health insurance, Internet service, and even my credit cards. Everything was paid automatically, so I've never paid a single dime in late fees.

Most companies make it easy to set up bill pay because it means they will always get paid. It also means you'll avoid paying late fees.

This is the beauty (and power!) of using automation to manage your money. It takes the discipline out of building wealth because you never have to remember to save, invest, and pay your bills. Once everything is set up, it just happens.

The great thing about using financial automation is you don't have to earn a big salary to take advantage of the benefits. Automated tools are available to all of us, regardless of our salaries. If you have a bank account, you have everything you need to build wealth and stay out of debt automatically.

If you think this sounds complicated, then don't worry. By the end of this chapter, you will know exactly how to set up simple, repeatable automated routines to ensure your money is saved, invested, and spent exactly as it should be.

Here is how it works:

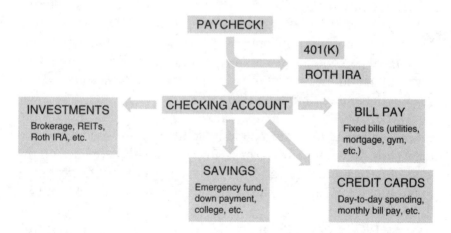

Imagine for a moment what it would be like for all this to happen—automatically. Without you having to lift a finger. You get paid. Then, you save, invest, and pay all your bills on a schedule without thinking about it.

Note: In the diagram above, I've included Roth IRA twice (once before the money hits your checking account and another after, inside the 'INVESTMENTS' box on the left). While some employers will automatically fund your Roth IRA from your paycheck, others won't, requiring a manual transfer to your Roth IRA from your checking account.

What Should You Automate?

I'm a big fan of automating as much as possible because I dislike sitting down and paying bills manually. (I also can't be trusted to remember to do it!) I'm naturally forgetful, so using automated systems has made my life much easier. Today, I automate as much as I can so I never have to think about saving, investing, and paying bills.

Here are some examples of things to automate:

- Utility bills;
- Mortgage or rent;
- Charitable donations;
- Credit card bills (maybe!);
- College savings plans: 529s;
- Loan repayments: car, student loans, etc.;
- Long-term retirement contributions: 401(k)s, etc.;
- Money transfers: emergency fund, investments, etc.;
- Memberships: gym, magazines, streaming services, etc.

But wait! Be careful with auto bill pay systems.

Even though you automatically pay your monthly bills such as utilities and credit cards, always check your bills and statements every month. This way, you can catch any errors you would unknowingly pay for in your statement.

It also helps ensure you have enough in your checking account to cover the bill.

For instance, perhaps you had many unexpected expenses hit you all at once. Your car broke down, requiring a $1,500 repair. Your toilet backed up. That's another $500 to the plumber. Your air conditioner stopped working. Super, that's $1,700. In one month, you charged another $3,700 to your credit card.

If you aren't careful, you risk overdrawing your checking account if you automatically paid your credit card bill without realizing you charged so much extra that month. But if you check your statement, you can quickly transfer another thousand or two from your emergency fund sitting in a separate savings account straight from your bank's online system (this is why emergency funds are so important).

Quick and easy. And you avoid overdraft fees.

When Should Each Automation Happen?

Most of these automated processes occur once a month, usually a few days after you get paid. If you get a paycheck twice a month (or biweekly), transfer money and pay your bills toward the end of the month to ensure you have enough money in your checking account to cover the cumulative amount of all the transfers and bills.

For instance, assume you get paid on the 1st and the 15th of every month. Instead of running money transfers twice (once after each paycheck), I recommend always keeping a little extra money in your checking account, running the transfers, and paying all of your bills monthly around the same time each month.

This will likely make it simpler.

Give your second paycheck of the month at least a few business days to clear before running automatic withdrawals away from your checking account. This allows time to clear up any mistakes or delays in depositing your paycheck into your account.

You might set the 20th of every month as your automation day. You transfer money into your separate savings account to fund your savings goals on that day. You also pay your fixed monthly bills on that day (your cell phone, streaming services, etc.), your credit card statement, and send money to your investment accounts (Roth IRA, brokerage, etc.).

The primary exception to this is bills that have different due dates. If you have a bill or any other financial obligation that must be addressed before the 20th of the month, adjust accordingly by making separate payments or transfers.

For those who get paid once a month, the same philosophy applies. If you get paid on the 1st, wait until at least the 5th or 6th to let your paycheck clear and become available in your checking account before transferring money and paying your bills.

How to Set Up Financial Automation

Most money transfers and automatic bill payments you can set up yourself by logging into the bank's or company's online system.

Here are a few examples of financial automation you can likely do yourself:

Transfer to a savings account: Log into your savings account and set up an automatic transfer from your checking account to your savings account. You will need to verify that you own the checking account. Sometimes, this requires you to verify two small arbitrary deposits of less than a dollar from your savings bank into your checking account (the savings bank will withdraw these deposits after verification).

Once you've verified your checking account, set up a monthly transfer for a set amount every month. You'll pick the day that you want the transfer to happen. Remember that if the date you choose falls on a weekend or holiday, the bank may not perform the transfer until the next business day.

Transfer to an investment account: Similar to transferring into savings, log into your investment account and set up a transfer from your checking (or savings) account to your investment account. Again, you will be asked to verify the account you're transferring from.

Automatic bill pay: Log into the company's online system to set up automatic bill payments. You will likely need to read and agree to the company's terms of service before setting up auto bill pay to authorize their system to draft your account. Some companies will give you a choice to pay your bill on a certain date of the month or immediately after your bill has been issued.

Employer-sponsored 401(k) and/or Roth IRA: Talk to your company's human resources or payroll department to set up auto deductions from your paycheck to fund your long-term retirement accounts such as a 401(k) and Roth IRA. You will likely need to sign paperwork before the company can authorize the payroll deduction. In addition, you will need to decide what percent of your paycheck should be deducted. I recommend contributing at least 20% of your paycheck to long-term retirement investment accounts if you can, or at the very least, the company match.

More details about 401(k)s and Roth IRAs and how much to contribute to these accounts in Habit #6.

Take Action: Here's How to Start with Financial Automation

Step 1: Make a list of all your accounts. First, list every online account you have for your money. This includes utility companies, investments, banks, credit cards, etc. Be sure you know how to log in to each of them. This also should include your employer's payroll system. Ask your employer if you are unsure what automatic savings and investing tools they offer.

Step 2: Connect them. Link your accounts together by logging into each account and adding your checking or savings account. This is the account that money will be pulled *from*. For instance, you might link your checking account to your cell phone bill to make sure your cell phone bill is paid in full each month.

Step 3: Establish savings/payment schedule. Lastly, set up each transfer and payment. Decide what day of the month will be your automation day, and use that day to automatically pay your bills and fund your savings and investment goals. If your employer offers a 401(k) or any other long-term investment opportunity, use payroll deductions to make this process easy and repeatable.

Step 4: Avoid overdraft penalties. To avoid overdraft penalties, set a calendar reminder each month before your automatic payments happen to ensure you have enough money in your bank account to cover all of your monthly bills.

Habit #6
Millionaires Invest (A Lot)

Also known as *making money while you sleep*, investing is the primary way people become millionaires. It's 100x tougher to build wealth if you don't invest.

I'm sure you hear that a lot. "You need to invest!" But you might not realize how important investing is in building wealth. And not just a little wealth, substantial wealth that can be passed down to your children and your children's children.

Why is investing so darn important?

The story begins with our good friend, *compound interest.*

Compound interest is a way to earn interest not only on the initial amount of money you save or invest but also on the interest you earn over time.

Wait, what?

If that was confusing, don't worry. It helps to consider an example.

Let's say you invest $1,000, and your rate of return over the subsequent year was 5%. In this case, you would earn $50 in interest in the first year.

The math looks like this: $1000 \times 0.05 = 50$.

As a result, you would have $1,050 after year one. Pretty cool, huh? You just made $50 without having to do anything but invest that initial $1,000.

Now, consider this question: How much money would you have after the second year, assuming the same 5% interest rate?

It stands to reason that you would earn another $50 the second year, bringing your two-year total to $1,100, doesn't it? **But that's the wrong answer.** After the second year, you would earn *more than $50* due to the power of compounding.

Here's why. The first year began with our $1,000 initial investment. But the second year begins with $1,050; the amount we have after our 5% return is factored into the equation. So year two ends with $1,102.50. We earned $52.50 during the second year, not just $50, because we started the year with $1,050.

The math looks like this: $1050 \times 0.05 = \$52.50$.

This process of earning interest on both the principal amount and the interest earned in previous years continues over time and can result in significant growth in your savings or investment over the long term.

I can hear your question now. "But Steve, $50 a year isn't a lot of money. How does this help us build wealth?"

There are two additional factors at play when we talk about how investing helps us become millionaires:

1. We aren't just investing once, and that's it;
2. We are investing with a multi-year time horizon.

What does this mean?

In our example, we made a one-time investment of $1,000, and that's it. But in practice, this isn't how investing happens. We keep investing more money with every paycheck. And we do it for many, many years.

For instance, let's go back to our earlier example. Instead of investing $1,000 once, let's add $100 to our initial investment of $1,000 every month. Over 10 years with an annual rate of return of 5 percent, we're looking at over $16,000!

In 20 years, it's over $42,300. After a 40-year career of investing $100 a month with a 5 percent rate of return, our investment is worth $152,000. We're in the money!

The good news doesn't stop there. We assumed a relatively conservative 5 percent rate of return. Historically, investors enjoy much higher returns when investing in the stock market. For example, The S&P 500 has returned an annualized average return of 11.88 percent since its inception in 1957.

If we were to rerun the math on our 40-year career with our $1,000 initial investment and invest $100 a month using an 11.88% rate of return, we're sitting on **$979,500**.

That's almost $1 million dollars!

Remember, we only put in $49,000 of our own money over those 40 years.

Welcome to the incredible power of compound interest!

Now that we've talked about why investing is important (and how it gets you rich), let's take a look at the easiest ways to invest to become a millionaire.

Believe it or not, investing is easy (it's not about picking and choosing stocks). It's also not just for the rich. And you don't need an investment advisor or a "stock guy" to design a simple money-making investment portfolio.

You don't need to pour over company's financial statements to invest. You don't even need to know what a yield is, or what "price-to-earnings ratio" means. Those are terms that self-proclaimed stock gurus and investment advisors throw out to make it seem as if investing were difficult. In truth, it's not. Investing is one of the easiest things you can do.

Nearly anyone can invest and start earning compound interest over time, and for the rest of this chapter, I will show you how it's done.

For the vast majority of millionaires, their investment portfolios are made up of stocks, bonds, and real estate.

Stocks

When you buy a share of stock, you're buying a stake in a company. When the company does well, the value of each share of stock increases, which means you just earned interest (or "capital gains") on the stock that you own.

In general, stocks are considered higher risk because the value of the shares you buy are influenced mainly by the performance of that company. If the company doesn't do well, the value of the stock you own will go down. In addition, the price of stocks can fluctuate wildly, especially in the short term. This volatility can make it difficult to predict how much money you will make or lose on an investment.

However, higher risk also means higher reward when stocks do well.

There are two primary ways to buy stock. You can buy shares of stock from individual companies such as Amazon, Google or Microsoft. Or you can invest in index funds, which are premade collections of stocks and bonds from different companies broadly diversified. In general, I encourage you to invest in index funds instead of individual stocks because picking and choosing companies to invest in contains a lot of risk.

Index funds distribute the risk, and this is what we call *diversification*. By investing in a larger collection of companies through an index fund, we reduce the chances of losing all of our money in the event a company collapses. We will talk more about index funds a little later in this chapter. But for now, know that they make investing easy.

Bonds

A bond is like an IOU that a company or government gives to people who loan them money. When you buy a bond, you are lending money to the company or government that issued the bond. In return, the company or government promises to pay you back the amount you lent, plus some extra money called interest, after a certain period of time.

This period of time is usually several years, like 2, 5, or 10, which means you won't get your money back until the bond "matures," or "expires." If you choose to withdraw your money before the bond matures, you will pay steep fees and penalties (in other words, don't do it).

The advantage of bonds is they drastically reduce risk. There are no guarantees with bonds, but the only way a bond won't be paid back is if a company defaults on the bond, which is a big deal. If you buy a government bond, the government would need to default on the bond, which isn't very likely to happen (they'll just print more money). While there are no guarantees, a bond is about as close to one as you'll get.

In general, bonds are attractive to rich people and older people, for two reasons.

1. Rich people want to preserve their wealth, and bonds do that by reducing the risk of asset depreciation if the stock market drops (as it did recently in 2008 and also in 2022).
2. Older people like the idea of almost guaranteed income. Without a full-time job, switching over from riskier stocks to less risky bonds will help grandma and grandpa design a dependable lifestyle with a fixed income.

Index Funds

Index funds are like the "easy button" of investing. Index funds have been around since 1975 when Vanguard founder John Bogle introduced the concept, and they've been a staple of many a millionaire's investment portfolio for decades.

Don't just take my word for it. Warren Buffett is widely considered one of the best investors in the history of the stock market. He once said, "A low-cost index fund is the most sensible equity investment for the great majority of investors."

An index fund is a fund that tracks an index, such as the Dow Jones Industrial Average or the S&P 500. An "index" in the stock market collectively tracks the performance of a group of company stock. Stock market indices are used by investors to track the overall performance of the stock market, as well as to compare the performance of different sectors of the market. They are also used by financial analysts to create investment strategies and to make recommendations to clients.

For instance, the three most common indices are the Dow Jones Industrial Average (DJIA), S&P 500, and the Nasdaq Composite index.

The DJIA tracks the performance of 30 blue-chip companies. Blue-chip companies are well-recognized, long-established, and financially sound companies that publicly trade stocks on the stock market. A few examples of blue-chip companies include Coca-Cola, Nike, Walmart, Chevron, and McDonald's.

The S&P 500 tracks the performance of 500 large-cap companies. Large-cap refers to companies worth more than $10 billion. Large-cap companies include Apple, Microsoft, Amazon, and Alphabet, who is Google's parent company.

The Nasdaq Composite tracks the performance of all stocks listed on the Nasdaq stock exchange.

To own an index fund, you invest in a fund that tracks a specific market index, such as the S&P 500 or the Dow Jones Industrial Average. When you buy shares of an index fund, you are essentially buying a small piece of ownership in all of the companies that make up the index. This means that your investment will rise and fall with the overall market, but it will not be as heavily impacted by the performance of any one company.

The advantages of index funds are attractive to many investors. Most index funds are low cost because they don't require highly paid fund managers to pick and choose stocks and bonds for the index. They are passively managed and offered by investment firms such as Vanguard, Fidelity, Goldman Sachs, and many others.

In addition, the built-in diversification of index funds reduces risk exposure to the investor. If one or two companies perform poorly, it likely won't pull down the overall performance of the index fund.

Lastly, index funds do not require the investor to manually select companies to invest in. Instead, the companies are selected based on the tracked index, for instance, the S&P 500.

In case you're wondering, the S&P 500 is a stock market index that tracks the performance of the 500 largest publicly traded companies in the United States. The S&P 500 includes a wide range of industries, including technology, health care, financial services, energy, and consumer goods. To many experts, the S&P 500 is a leading indicator of the performance of the US economy and is widely used as a benchmark for investment portfolios.

Targeted Retirement Funds

Also known as "target date" funds, these funds are great options for investors who never want to touch their investments over their working careers.

The idea behind targeted retirement funds is simple. Younger investors can afford to be more risky (because they have more time to recover any losses) while older investors, especially those close to retirement, are less risky. As the investor approaches their retirement date, the target date fund automatically adjusts the investment mix to reduce risk by shifting a greater portion of the assets into bonds, which typically offer lower returns but are less volatile. We discussed bonds earlier in this chapter.

Your job is to pick the year you think that you might retire.

For example, let's say you want to retire in 2056, and you're a hands-off investor who wants to build wealth without having to pick and choose stocks. You might choose the "Target Retirement 2056 Fund" from an investment company such as Vanguard or Fidelity. The 2056 fund would slowly transition from stocks to bonds over the years until 2056, when it would hold the largest percentage of less risky bonds.

Targeted retirement funds are a convenient and simple way for investors to build a diversified investment portfolio without having to constantly monitor and make risk-related adjustments. However, it's important to carefully review the investment mix and fees associated with these funds, as well as any minimum initial investment, as they can vary widely between different providers and may not be suitable for all investors depending on their specific financial goals and risk tolerance.

Exchange-Traded Funds (ETFs)

Exchange-traded funds, or ETFs, are similar to index funds in that they track the performance of particular indexes, such as the S&P 500. However, unlike index funds, ETFs can be bought and sold directly on the stock exchange rather than through an investment firm, which is required with index funds.

While index funds can require minimum investments, ETFs typically don't because they are bought and sold as whole shares, similar to buying a share of stock. In addition, many ETFs are designed to track more focused sectors of the market (rather than broad indexes), giving investors more control over what they invest in.

Like index funds, ETFs are diversified, passively managed, and require low fees, making them great options for investors of all ages. Whether you're a 20-year-old just starting out in the workforce or a grandparent, ETFs are good options if you're looking for convenience, ease, and maximum growth potential.

ETFs have become quite popular in recent years, including:

SPY (SPDR S&P 500): This ETF tracks the S&P 500 index, which is a benchmark for the broader US stock market.

QQQ (Invesco QQQ Trust): This ETF tracks the Nasdaq 100 index, which includes the 100 largest nonfinancial companies listed on the Nasdaq stock exchange.

IVV (iShares Core S&P 500 ETF): Similar to SPY, this ETF tracks the S&P 500 index.

VTI (Vanguard Total Stock Market ETF): This ETF tracks the CRSP US Total Market Index, which includes nearly all publicly traded stocks in the US.

DIA (SPDR Dow Jones Industrial Average ETF): This ETF tracks the Dow Jones Industrial Average, which includes 30 large-cap US companies.

Mutual Funds

A mutual fund is a type of investment vehicle that pools money together from multiple investors to purchase a portfolio of assets including stocks and bonds. Each investor owns shares of the mutual fund, which represent a portion of the total assets held by the fund.

Mutual funds are actively managed by fund managers. Essentially, fund managers make decisions on your behalf about buying and selling. Good fund managers can make mutual funds quite lucrative. The downside is those human fund managers make mutual funds pricier than passive index funds, and humans usually underperform market indexes such as the S&P 500.

While mutual funds are a convenient way to diversify your investments without picking and choosing stocks and bonds yourself, cheaper (and passive!) investing options (such as an index fund) make mutual funds less attractive.

Real Estate

A lot of millionaires built their wealth by investing in real estate. In fact, billionaire investor Andrew Carnegie once said that 90 percent of millionaires got their wealth by investing in real estate. Real estate has made a lot of people very rich.

Don't see yourself being a landlord? Don't worry. Real estate investing takes on a slew of different forms. You don't need to be a landlord to invest in real estate.

One of the easiest ways to start investing in real estate without becoming a landlord is to invest in REITs, or real estate investment trusts. A REIT is a type of company that owns or finances income-producing real estate assets. REITs are required to pay out profits to shareholders in the form of dividends. A dividend represents a portion of earnings that is sent, usually by check, to shareholders. Similar to ETFs, REITs are publicly traded on major stock exchanges and offer investors the opportunity to invest in real estate without owning or managing the properties.

REITs are very popular today because they offer investors an easy, hands-off way to invest in real estate. Some REITs own equity in physical properties while others invest in mortgages and other real estate–related debts. Many REITs invest in both.

Other real estate investors buy vacant parcels of land, hold them, and resell them in the future for a profit. Vacant land investing is a very long-term type of investment and requires enough capital to buy parcels for cheap. Most mortgage lenders won't lend on vacant land, requiring investors to have enough cash on hand for the entire purchase.

And yes, some real estate investors buy homes and rent them out. This can be especially lucrative if the investor finds a cheaper home in need of repairs and can do most of the repairs themselves, saving thousands of dollars in labor costs.

Often, the best income-producing residential properties are multifamily buildings such as apartments, duplexes, and townhouses. These buildings are more expensive to buy and maintain, but landlords get multiple rent payments every month. Alternatively, multifamily REITs let investors invest in more expensive townhomes or condos without having to buy and maintain the building. The rent is paid out to investors as dividends.

Before we move on from real estate, I would be remiss if I didn't mention this point: your home is typically not a good real estate investment. While it's true that you can make money with your primary residence, this happens less often than you would think after factoring in all the costs of homeownership. Add up everything and the true cost of ownership is substantially higher than the purchase price.

For instance, consider this table of expenses that homeowners pay (that renters would typically not pay):

Down payment	The initial payment made at the time of the purchase, which is usually 10–20%
Homeowners insurance	Insurance that protects the homeowner from financial loss due to damage or theft
Private mortgage insurance (PMI)	Insurance required by some lenders if the down payment is less than 20%
Property taxes	Taxes paid to the government based on the assessed value of the property
Maintenance and repairs	The cost of repairing and maintaining the home, such as fixing leaks
Homeowners association (HOA) fees	Fees paid to an HOA for the maintenance and upkeep of shared amenities
Pest control	The cost of removing pest infestations such as termites, bees, and other insects and critters

When combined, the additional fees and responsibilities associated with homeownership will make the price of your home more costly than what you had originally paid, making your primary residence a less attractive investment. For instance, over 10 years, the true cost of a $300,000 could easily be $500,000 or more.

In addition, most homeowners can't use the "buy low, sell high" investment philosophy with their primary home as you might with stocks. In other words, it would be difficult for a homeowner to sell their home when the market is high, but avoid paying an equally high price to find another home, essentially canceling out any gains from the home sale.

After all, we all need to live somewhere, don't we?

I'm certainly not criticizing homeownership, as I'm a big fan of it. However, understand your true cost of ownership before considering your home a real estate investment.

Traditional 401(k)

The 401(k) is one of the most common investment vehicles millionaires use to invest and build wealth for retirement. It allows employees to contribute a percentage of their pretax income to a tax-advantaged retirement account, which grows over time through investments in asset classes such as stocks, bonds, and mutual funds.

The 401(k) reduces your taxable income by the amount that you contribute, which is a great deal unless you enjoy paying more in taxes.

To illustrate, let's look at an example. Let's say you earn $80,000 in taxable income and you decide to contribute $10,000 to your 401(k) plan over the course of a year. Your total adjusted gross income for the year will be reduced to $70,000 (80,000 − 10,000), which means you will pay less in income taxes.

Assuming a marginal tax rate of 22 percent, your tax liability before contributing to the 401(k) would be around $11,000 (there are lots of factors that determine the exact amount that are outside the scope of this book!). However, after contributing $10,000 to your 401(k), your taxable income is reduced to $70,000, and your tax liability drops to $9,000, a savings of $2,000.

In this example, by contributing to your 401(k) plan, you were able to lower your tax bill by $2,000, which means you get to keep more of your hard-earned money (and less goes to Uncle Sam, a win-win). Additionally, the money you contribute to your 401(k) plan grows tax-deferred until you withdraw it in retirement, which can further increase your savings over time.

Tax-deferred means you only pay taxes on the gains when its withdrawn in retirement. It's a gem of an investment opportunity. No wonder so many millionaires use it!

Investing in a traditional 401(k) is a smart move for several reasons.

Reason #1: It allows you to enrich your retirement with consistent investing over your career while reducing your current tax burden.
Reason #2: Many employers will match a percentage of your contributions with their own money. This is essentially free money that can help your savings grow even faster.
Reason #3: Investing in a traditional 401(k) lets you enjoy the power of compound interest. Over time, your investments can grow exponentially as the gains are reinvested, and you earn gains on your original investment as well as the returns.
Reason #4: Finally, it is also a convenient way to save for retirement because the contributions are automatically deducted from your paycheck through the power of automation (you learned about this in Habit #5). Automation helps you to stay on track with your money goals and can help ensure that you have enough money saved for a comfortable retirement.

There is a catch with the 401(k): Restrictions apply to withdrawing the money, and the government limits how much you can contribute per year without penalty. As of 2023, individuals can contribute up to $22,500 into their 401(k) accounts. Those over 50 years old can plop an additional $7,500 into their 401(k). The Internal Revenue Service changes the rules every year so always be sure to understand the limitations. Your employer can help you figure this out if you aren't sure.

Withdrawals can be made from your 401(k) when you reach 59½ and must be made when you reach 72 (known as Required Minimum Distributions, or RMDs). Don't take money out of your 401(k) before you reach 59½ or you'll face penalties that will eat into your capital gains.

Before we talk about Roth IRAs, I want to give another shout out to the match that some employers give to employees' 401(k) plans. Many employers will match a percentage of your income that you put in to your 401(k) with *their* money. That's right, that's 100 percent free money from your employer deposited straight into your 401(k). The catch is you also have to contribute to your 401(k) in order to be eligible for the match. If your employer offers a match, make sure you're contributing enough to get the full match.

Roth IRA

If you like to avoid taxes, then the Roth IRA is your ideal investment account.

A Roth IRA (Individual retirement account) is a post-tax retirement plan that lets employees invest money for retirement. This means it won't reduce your taxable income like the 401(k), but you won't pay any taxes when you withdraw this money in retirement (provided you've had your Roth IRA account for more than five years). It's tax-free growth for your entire career. What a country!

Like the 401(k), the government has placed restrictions on how much you can contribute to your Roth IRA, and when money can be withdrawn without penalty. As with the 401(k), you can begin making withdrawals from your Roth IRA at 59½. If you withdraw earlier, you'll need to pay a penalty. As of 2023, that penalty is 10%.

The Internal Revenue Service only allows $6,500 in contributions per year, or $7,500 if you're over 50. It also won't let high income earners (think over $153,000 for single head of households or $218,000 for joint filers) contribute to a Roth IRA at all.

There are no Required Minimum Distributions with the Roth IRA, so you can let your money continue to build as long as you want.

Health Savings Accounts

Not many people know how powerful a health savings account is. But since you're reading this book, congratulations! You will.

Health savings accounts, or HSAs, are great options for further long-term investment growth. These accounts are designed to let people set money aside for qualified medical expenses such as health care deductibles, hearing aids, dental care, flu shots, medications, and so forth.

HSAs offer a triple tax benefit:

Tax benefit #1: HSAs are pretax savings accounts, which means every dollar contributed to an HSA lowers taxable income, just like the 401(k).

Tax benefit #2: Your HSA will grow tax-free.

Tax benefit #3: Your contributions can be withdrawn at any time tax-free for qualified medical expenses.

But it gets even better. After turning 65, your HSA turns into a traditional 401(k). This means any remaining money in your HSA can be withdrawn and spent on *anything* without restrictions or penalties after your 65th birthday. Pretty good deal, eh?

There's only one catch. Any money used for non-qualified medical expenses after 65 will be taxed as income. However, that's a small price to pay for reducing your taxable income and setting up a sizable nest egg in case of health-related expenses.

Note that HSAs require high deductible health plans, so they won't be right (or even available) for everyone. For instance, if you pay for medical expenses often, it could be safer to keep this money set aside in a savings account where it is 100% safe.

Cryptocurrencies

If I had a dollar every time someone told me that "crypto is the future," I'd be a millionaire all over again. Of course, this was also back when Bitcoin experienced its unnatural and meteoric rise in 2021 and crypto was in the news almost every day. Strangely, I'm hearing from those folks less and less these days.

I am not a fan of cryptocurrencies. I wasn't a fan back in 2021, and I'm certainly not today. I am unconvinced of their long-term viability and certainly don't think an asset such as Bitcoin will ever again experience its superhuman growth like it did. However, that doesn't mean crypto can't represent a portion of your overall investment strategy.

Crypto is an asset class just like anything else we've talked about in this chapter.

If you're unclear what crypto is, here's a brief lesson.

A cryptocurrency is a type of digital currency that uses encryption techniques to regulate the generation of units of currency and ledgers to verify the transfer of funds.

An attractive element of cryptocurrencies is in how they are controlled. Unlike the US dollar, which is governed by the Federal Reserve, digital currencies operate independently of a central bank and can be used to purchase goods and services online or exchanged for other currencies, including traditional currencies such as dollars or euros. However, buying and selling goods and services with digital currencies isn't exactly common even though crypto currencies have been around for many years.

In simpler terms, it's like virtual money that can be used to buy things online or traded for other types of money. Think of it like Monopoly money. It's unique because it's decentralized, meaning no single entity controls it, and it uses cryptography to secure transactions and control the creation of new units. Creating new cryptocurrencies requires substantial investment and computing power.

Most crypto investors use the US dollar (or their own country's currency) to buy and hold a digital currency, hoping it increases in value. The cryptocurrency can then be sold and exchanged for another currency or used for goods and services.

Popular examples of cryptocurrencies include Bitcoin, Ethereum, and Litecoin.

Active vs. Passive Investing

According to one report, nearly 80 percent of active fund managers underperform an index such as the S&P 500. Though nearly every active investor believes they are in the 20 percent minority, the numbers show they probably aren't.

The difference between active and passive investing can cost you a lot of money. Let's take a look at the major differences between active and passive investing.

Active investing: Active investors actively manage their portfolio of stocks, bonds, and other assets by picking and choosing companies to invest in. They typically buy and sell stocks and bonds much more frequently than passive investors. They do this by buying companies they think will do well and avoiding companies they believe won't. They may also use complex investment strategies, such as derivatives or short-selling, to achieve their investment objectives. Active investing requires a significant amount of time and effort, as well as a deep understanding of financial markets.

Passive investing: In contrast, passive investors use index funds and ETFs to automatically spread their money throughout the market without manually selecting stocks and typically perform better than their active counterparts. The goal of passive investing is to match the overall performance of the market. Passive investing takes much less time than active investing, making it an attractive and easy strategy for a lot of investors.

Is it impossible for active investors to "beat the market"? Certainly not. Many active investors outperform the S&P 500 and other indexes. However, it is more likely that you won't unless you have a deep understanding of markets and financial strategies and are willing to accept substantially higher risk. Unless you love paying attention to yields and price-to-earnings ratios, passive investing is usually the better option.

The "Passive-first" Investment Strategy

Many investors who want to pick and choose stocks but also want the benefits of passive investing utilize a blended approach that mixes the two investing philosophies. I like to call this the "passive-first" investment strategy.

To use the passive-first strategy, keep the majority of your investments in passive index funds and ETFs and then devote a set percentage to active investments. The percentage you use to actively invest will depend heavily on your risk tolerance and your overall investment goals and values.

The higher your risk tolerance, the higher percentage of your investments you'll actively invest. The less risky you are, the less you'll actively invest. In general, devoting 20 percent or more of your investments to actively invest is higher risk.

For instance, many passive-first investors use a 90/10 split between passive and active investing, which strikes a reasonable risk balance (not too risky, but not low risk). Keep 90% of your investments in passive index funds and have a little fun with the remaining 10% picking your own stocks. Even if things don't go well with the 10%, it won't destroy your wealth.

It's important not to drastically boost your active investing percentage because you had a good year. It's great making more money than the S&P 500 index, but remember it only takes a single bad investment to wipe out the majority of your gains. And as we've discussed in this book, passive investing tends to outperform active.

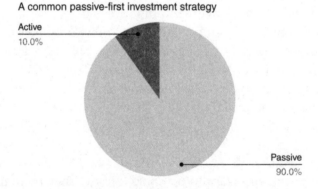

A common passive-first investment strategy

Active
10.0%

Passive
90.0%

Both active and passive investors can become millionaires. For the vast majority of us, you are more likely to join the double-comma club by adopting a passive or passive-first strategy. All you need to do is invest. Then, let the market do what it does best.

Long-term Investing Makes Millionaires

It's attractive to want to "get rich quick," isn't it? But if it were that easy, everybody would be doing it. You would already be a millionaire. So would your neighbor.

Building wealth takes time, and this is especially true in the stock market. The S&P 500 has returned a historic annualized average of 11.8% since its inception in 1957. The longer you're invested, the better your chances of building wealth.

Here, let me prove it to you.

If you invested $100 in the S&P 500 back in 1990, reinvested all of your dividends and didn't invest another dollar since then, you would be sitting on a stockpile of $2,390. That's an average return of $10% every year. As we learned earlier in this chapter, the power of compounding helps our wealth grow exponentially.

This includes the market slump in the early 2000s, the devastating market collapse in 2009 and the fall from grace the S&P 500 experienced in 2022. Even with all these substantial market dips, the index still returned over 10%, on average.

This is why time in the market beats timing the market.

The longer you stay invested, the better your chances of building wealth (dollar-cost averaging helps here, and we'll talk more about that in the next section).

I love illustrating important points with examples, so let's use another one here.

Let's consider two hypothetical investors—David and Lisa.

David is a short-term investor who prefers to make quick profits by buying and selling stocks within a few days or weeks (hint: this is active investing!). He spends a lot of time monitoring the stock market, reading quarterly earnings reports (yawn!), and making frequent stock trades to take advantage of short-term market fluctuations.

Lisa, on the other hand, is a long-term investor who believes in holding onto stocks for an extended period, typically years or even decades. She invests in index funds and ETFs because she doesn't want the risk associated with picking and choosing stocks, and she rarely makes any changes to her portfolio.

Over time, it's likely that Lisa will make more money than David. This is because short-term investing involves a lot of risk, and it is unlikely to consistently beat the market. Short-term traders sometimes make a quick profit on a trade or two, but they are also susceptible to market fluctuations, which can lead to significant losses.

In contrast, long-term investors such as Lisa benefit from the power of compounding. By holding onto high-quality stocks for an extended period, they can benefit from the steady growth of the companies they invest in. Traders such as Lisa will be exposed to down markets and recessions, but as history has consistently proven, markets tend to go up.

Remember, long-term investors benefit from the rock-solid fact that the stock market tends to rise over time. By holding onto a diversified portfolio of stocks, they can participate in the growth of the overall market, which has historically provided returns of around 8–10% per year.

Overall, while short-term investing may provide occasional quick gains, the long-term investor like Lisa will likely end up making more money over time by staying invested for the long haul.

Why Dollar-cost Averaging Works

You've already learned how much easier index funds and ETFs make it to invest. But what if I told you there was a way to make it *easier still*?

Welcome to dollar-cost averaging (and to Easy Street).

Dollar-cost averaging (DCA) is a straightforward investment strategy in which assets such as stocks and bonds are bought at regular intervals, regardless of the asset's price. I used this investment strategy my whole life because it's easy and effective.

For example, suppose you want to invest 20% of your salary. You get paid every two weeks. Using the DCA strategy, you invest 20% of each paycheck rather than making a lump sum investment every month (or even just once a year). And you *definitely* don't try to time market conditions by dumping a bunch of money into the market when you think it's at its lowest point. Unless you're lucky, that doesn't work.

To make this process even easier, you might use payroll deductions available from your employer to regularly make these investments, or an automatic bank transfer every two weeks. It always happens like clockwork. No need to remember.

While I love the DCA strategy and still use it to this day, there is one instance where it might not be your best course of action. Let's say you get a big financial windfall, like an inheritance. You might think using DCA will mitigate the risk of investing a large sum of money at a single point in time, as it spreads out the investment over time and can help smooth the impact of market volatility. However, this doesn't always work.

For instance, using the DCA strategy after a windfall, you would invest a $50,000 inheritance regularly over time rather than dumping the entire sum into the market at once. However, Vanguard found that lump sum investing beat dollar-cost averaging about two thirds of the time.[1] This is because the market usually goes up (but of course, not always!). Investing the entire $50,000 into the market at once means that your money is invested for a longer period of time. As we've learned in this chapter, the longer your money is invested, the greater the potential return.

If you have a big pile of money to invest, you might be better off lump-sum investing, especially if the market is stable or going up.

DCA is a great way to make regular investment contributions over time, and most of us are already doing this with employer auto deductions or automated bank transfers. But if you have a bunch of money that you want to invest, it's likely best to invest it all at once.

Are Stocks Down? Don't Panic!

One of the best ways to lose money in the stock market is by panic-selling when the market is down. Selling when stocks are falling locks in your losses. When you sell an investment at a loss, you're banking on the investment continuing to decrease in value.

However, history has shown that markets do eventually rebound after downturns. If you sell during a down market, you'll likely miss out on the recovery.

On the contrary, a down market can be the perfect opportunity to buy more stocks because stocks are "on sale," or cheaper than they were just a few months or years ago.

It's natural to feel a little anxiety when the market is down. However, it's important to remember that emotions cloud your judgment and lead to poor investment decisions. If you're feeling uncertain or pessimistic about the market, it's a good idea to take a hands-off approach and avoid making any big financial decisions and come back to your investments when you're feeling more rational.

Take Action: Here's What You Need to Do

Step 1: Knock out your 401(k) and Roth IRA. If your employer offers a 401(k) or Roth IRA, start investing a portion of your paycheck. Most employers offer payroll deductions, which makes it easy and straightforward to fund these accounts. If your employer matches a percentage of your income in your 401(k), contribute enough to get the entire match (remember, it's free money).

Step 2: Open a brokerage account. If you don't have access to a 401(k) or Roth IRA (or if you're a go-getter and want to invest more), open a brokerage account at an investment firm such as Vanguard. Use automated bank transfers to invest every month automatically. Depending on your level of risk, you might decide to pick and choose individual stocks or, if you're less risky (and want to outperform active investors), opt for ETFs, index funds, and targeted retirement accounts. If you're unsure of your options, most investment firms have advisors that you can speak with to determine what investment options are right for you.

Step 3: Commit to investing 20% of your income. The more you invest, the more you can make, but only if you take a long-term approach. Aim to invest at least 20% of each paycheck in long-term investments. If you aren't there yet, that's okay. This is a process. The point is to develop a plan and stick to it. Invest what you can today, and then slowly increase the amount you invest as you progress in your career with raises and job promotions.

Note

1. Berger, R. "Dollar Cost Averaging vs. Lump Sum Investing—How to Decide." Forbes (2021). https://www.forbes.com/sites/robertberger/2021/02/12/dollar-cost-averaging-vs-lump-sum-investing-how-to-decide/?sh=63f7a667c500.

Habit #7

Millionaires Save for Emergencies

I f there's one thing that destroys wealth, it's a huge unexpected bill. Not only do financial emergencies eat away at our wealth, but they spiral us into a cycle of debt that can be extremely tough to escape.

Imagine that your roof springs a leak. There's water pouring in through the ceiling, dripping on your television or computer. The *new* computer you bought last week.

"Crap! Crap! Crap!" you say. This is going to be expensive!

You put a couple of buckets under the drip to catch the water, get on the phone and beg a contractor to look at the damage. Miraculously, you found a contractor available the same day you call (I know, this never happens, but stick with me here), and they come over, inspect the leak, and quote you a price of $20,000 for the repair.

The $20,000 needs to cover the damage to your ceiling, new electrical wiring, and drywall—not to mention the repairs to your roof, plus labor.

You have no choice (and little time to get another quote). Your roof is leaking and needs to be fixed ASAP. You accept the quote and use your credit card to put half down for the contractor to start work. Boom, that's $10,000 on your card.

By the end of the job, assuming no additional expenses, you're looking at more than $20,000 on your credit card, which is 10x more than you normally would spend.

What happens now?

Scenario #1: You have a three-month emergency fund, so this isn't a problem. You casually log into your savings account where you keep your emergency fund, transfer over $20,000 into your primary checking account, and pay off your credit card bill. Then, you commit to putting $200 a month back into your savings account to build your emergency savings again. No big deal, you tell yourself. Stuff happens, and that's why you have a rainy day fund.

After making the money transfer, you grab a cup of tea and catch up on the latest few Property Brothers episodes from your comfortable (and dry) living room.

Scenario #2: You don't have enough money to pay off the credit card at the end of the month, so you carry a balance into the next month. You pay $3,000 off, leaving at least $17,000 (remember you probably have other expenses on that credit card, too) at a 21 percent interest rate. Next month, you pay $3,500, bringing your card's balance down to around $13,500. Another 21 percent interest charge. And the next month. . .

It takes you six months to fully pay off the credit card. After paying it off, you realize you wasted hundreds of dollars in interest payments because you let that credit card balance sit on your card for almost a half-year.

Okay, you probably get the idea. You want to be in scenario #1. Whether it's a roof repair, an auto accident, a medical bill, or an unexpected job loss, put yourself into the position of having enough cash available to take care of unexpected financial mayhem.

This is what millionaires do because they know living without a little extra money set aside is ripe for a financial catastrophe (not to mention a heck of a lot of stress).

If you don't have money set aside (or you're afraid it might not be enough), here is how to start building your very first emergency fund.

How Much Should You Save?

The biggest question with emergency funds is how big it should be. Aim to keep three to six months of living expenses in your emergency fund to give yourself a nice financial cushion for a rainy day.

"But Steve," you might say. "The difference between three months and six months is huge! Which one should I follow?" Good question. Let's dive into that.

First, why is three months' living expenses the *minimum* you should save?

Because that's generally enough time to find another job if you lose yours. If you get fired tomorrow, your emergency fund keeps you afloat without losing your shirt (or something more important!). You have three months to find a new job.

However, there are several reasons why you might want to keep more than three months' worth of money in your emergency fund.

If you are less risk averse, then saving more money might help you sleep better at night, knowing you have a larger chunk of change at the ready. In addition, in single-income households with kids, a job loss can be a very significant event. Imagine if the major breadwinner loses his or her job with a family of four to feed. In that case, a six-month emergency fund provides a much larger financial cushion to use to keep food on the table and the lights on while finding a new job. In general, the larger your family, the bigger your emergency fund.

How to Set Up Your First Emergency Fund

Your goal is to keep at least three months of living expenses in a separate savings or money market account. You will never touch these emergency savings unless you need to cover an unexpected financial burden.

Your living expenses include everything that you spend money on during the month. This includes things such as your mortgage/

rent, utilities, gas, health insurance, cell phone, pet food, and child-care. Anything you spend money on, those are your living expenses.

If you spend $5,000 a month to maintain your lifestyle (from the house you live to the streaming services you subscribe to), then your goal is to set $15,000 aside. And remember, you're separating this money into a savings or money market account, not keeping it in your checking account where it's easy to spend accidentally.

Here is your three-step guide to creating your first emergency fund.

Step 1: Separate It

The last thing you want to do is combine all your savings together into your primary checking account. That money is too easy to accidentally (or on purpose) spend. Instead, put this cash into a savings or money market account.

Like storing chocolate in our pantry: If it's there, we will be tempted to take a piece! Let's not tempt ourselves.

We use an Ally savings account for our emergency fund.

We earn a small amount of interest on the money, and it's impossible to accidentally spend because that money is completely separated from our primary checking account. But it's also easy to access if we need it for unexpected expenses and emergencies.

Controversy alert: Some people prefer to invest their emergency savings in the stock market, arguing that keeping three months' worth of money is too much cash (as you recall, cash doesn't grow like money invested in the market).

I don't agree with this argument. You never want to be forced to sell stocks to pay an unexpected expense. First, you will owe taxes when you sell. And, you always want to fully control when you sell stock 100 percent of the time.

In addition, it's possible that the market will go down right before you need to use this money, slashing the available cash.

Your emergency *savings* is just that. It's not an investment. Keep that money safe from the market's ups and downs by stashing it in an interest-bearing savings account.

Step 2: Make It a Priority

If you don't have any money set aside for emergencies, then make it your priority. Building an emergency fund is more important than investing or paying off debt. Remember that emergencies cause debt.

Large unexpected expenses destroy wealth. But the more prepared we are to withstand an unexpected expense or job loss financially, the better our chances of pulling through without incurring credit card debt.

Over half of Americans can't cover a $1,000 emergency with their savings. That means they are charging these expenses to their credit cards and racking up high-interest credit card debt along the way.

If you cannot easily cover a $1,000 emergency without using a credit card or borrowing money, make your rainy day fund your #1 priority.

To help make this easy, use automated routines to build your emergency fund. We will discuss how to use automation more in Step 3 next.

Step 3: Use Automation to Make It Easy

If you've already read the chapter on automation (that was Habit #5), then you know I'm a huge fan of using automated routines to make money management easy. Using computers to automate repetitive tasks such as investing or saving money is a great way to make building your emergency fund easy.

Why is automation so important? Automation takes discipline out of the equation because computers won't forget to make a money transfer. But humans might! And most banks offer online systems that let us easily set up recurring monthly transfers, making the process of scheduling money transfers easy.

Log into your savings account and set up a monthly transfer from your checking account for an amount you're comfortable with (e.g. $100 a month). Note that this process will require you to link your primary checking account to your savings account so your savings bank can access the money you transfer every month.

Once the scheduled transfer is set up, it happens monthly without you lifting a finger. Slowly but surely, your emergency savings will build.

The automated system will never forget. Set it up once, and then forget it.

Remember that Rome wasn't built in a day, nor were six-month emergency funds. If you can only save $50 a month right now, that's fine. Save $50. Then, increase that savings rate when you can. Building your emergency savings is a marathon, not a sprint. The key is to start and stay consistent until you have three to six months of living expenses saved and ready to go (not that you ever want to use it).

Where Should You Keep Your Emergency Savings

As we've discussed, you should never invest your emergency fund in the stock market because you don't want to be forced to sell and incur income taxes to cover an unexpected expense. Instead, you only want to sell stocks on your terms.

There are several good places to keep your emergency savings.

Savings account: This is the simplest and most straightforward place to stash your rainy day fund. Your savings account is physically separated from your primary checking, which gives your money extra protection from being accidentally spent. If you want even extra protection, consider a savings account at a different bank than your primary checking account. This way you don't even see the account if you log in online, and it'll take a couple of extra days to transfer money, making it that much more difficult for you to steal from your emergency fund for a nonemergency.

Choose a "high-yield savings account," which means it is federally insured for up to $250,000 per person, so it's safe. And you'll get a little interest along the way, which will help your emergency fund grow a little bit over the months. Interest rates will vary greatly from bank to bank and will change periodically. I've seen some savings banks give as much as 5 to 6% (or more) interest and as little as just 0.01%.

Money market: Money market accounts, offered by banks and credit unions, are a type of bank account that typically offers higher interest rates than traditional savings accounts. However, they also require a higher minimum deposit and balance than savings accounts and sometimes restrict the number of monthly transactions you can make (in general, this shouldn't be a problem unless you have a lot of emergencies). Like savings accounts, money market accounts are FDIC-insured up to $250,000.

Certificate of deposit (CD): CDs are less attractive for your emergency fund but work for some people. While CDs can earn you more interest than a savings or money market account, they are also time-sensitive and restrict when you can withdraw your money without penalties.

Most CD terms range from one month to 10 or more years (e.g. a one-year CD), which is the amount of time you agree to keep your money in the CD. You will be penalized with fees if you try to take your money out of a CD before the expiration date.

As a result, a CD can be a good option for a portion of your emergency fund, but I recommend against keeping all of your emergency savings tied up in an account that you cannot access, without penalty, at any time. A CD is a better option if you are saving for something specific in the future, a five-year wedding anniversary trip to the Galápagos Island, for example.

What Is An Emergency?

Before we end this chapter, let's briefly discuss what constitutes an emergency. No, that TV you've been eying that finally goes on sale isn't an emergency!

An emergency is any unexpected event that requires a lot of quick cash.

For instance, that leaky roof from earlier in this chapter is a prime example of an emergency. You didn't expect that to happen, but it needs to be fixed.

A few other examples of emergencies include:

- **Pet expenses:** If you have a pet, you may need to use your emergency fund to cover the cost of unexpected medical expenses, such as if your pet gets injured or sick.
- **Losing your job:** If you lose your job, you may need to use your emergency fund to cover your living expenses until you find a new job.
- **Natural disasters:** Hurricanes, tornadoes, and other natural disasters strike at a moment's notice and may require quick money to perform repairs.
- **Getting into an accident:** Car repairs can be expensive, especially unexpected ones. Your emergency fund can help you cover the cost of repairs if your car breaks down.
- **Medical bills from an illness:** Unexpected medical expenses can be very expensive, even if you have health insurance. Your emergency fund can help you cover the cost of copays, deductibles, and other out-of-pocket expenses.

Case in point: My wife and I were driving home one evening in our Hyundai Sonata, and a jackrabbit darted out into the road and caused more than $2,000 worth of damage to the underside of our car. That's $2,000 from a jackrabbit! In other words, things happen, and sometimes those things require money you didn't anticipate spending. Our e-fund made this only an inconvenience rather than a financial burden.

This is exactly what your emergency fund is for.

Take Action: Here's What You Need to Do

Step 1: If you don't have an emergency fund, start one.
Open a savings account, and use that account to hold your
emergency fund. Then, set up an automatic bank transfer from your primary checking account to your savings
account and transfer in as much as you feel comfortable.
Your emergency savings will build over time, automatically. I love it when things are just easy.

Step 2: Don't steal from it! It might be tempting to "borrow"
a little from your emergency savings, but don't do it. This
money is earmarked for a true emergency, not for that
"Memorial Day extravaganza" sale at the car dealership.
When you steal from your emergency fund, you're stealing
from yourself. Pretend it's not there; only use it when you
have to.

Step 3: If you need it, use it. Believe it or not, some people
resist using their emergency fund because it took them so
long to build, and they've formed some sort of weird emotional connection to it. Don't! It's there for a reason. Don't
go into debt because you don't want to spend your savings.
That's why it's there. You might need to use your credit
card initially, and that's fine. Then, log into your savings
bank and transfer money straight to your credit card or to
your primary checking account and pay your credit card
bill from there.

Habit #8

Millionaires Create Their Own Luck

The word "luck" gets thrown around a lot. It seems like every time I talk about millionaires or wealthy people on social media, a segment of people invariably chalks up their success to luck. It's always just dumb luck.

Started a successful business? You probably had help from your parents.

Became a millionaire in their 30s? You probably just got an inheritance.

But strangely enough, I've never heard anyone say that Michael Jordan (one of the best and most popular NBA basketball players ever to play) just got lucky.

With few exceptions, we don't think of most sports stars as "lucky." We recognize the hard work and grueling daily practices they went through to make it to the pros and continue playing at a high level throughout their careers.

You know, an hour in the gym every day. Wind sprints at the end of practice. Getting yelled at by coaches for doing something wrong.

At Laney High School in Wilmington, North Carolina, Michael Jordan failed to make the varsity basketball team as a sophomore, which fueled his determination to improve.

Jordan spent thousands of hours honing his skills and working on his game. He would get up early and practice before school, participate in team practices, and then continue playing long after official practice sessions ended. His relentless dedication allowed him to earn a spot on the varsity team and eventually establish himself as an outstanding player.

It's fascinating to me that nobody considers pro sports players "lucky" to have made it to the pros, but when it comes to money and success in all other areas of life, suddenly, it's all about luck. They didn't earn it. They just got lucky or had rich parents.

Dave Ramsey found nearly 74 percent of millennials believe millionaires inherited their money. More than half of baby boomers believe the same thing. In other words, three-fourths of millennials want to believe that millionaires lucked into their money.

It was all pure chance. What a dreadfully poor mindset.

I looked all over for research and studies on the topic of money, inheritance, and luck, and what I found was overwhelming. **The numbers show that most millionaires are self-made.** That means they didn't just fall into their money. It wasn't inheritance. In fact, a fascinatingly large percentage of millionaires never earned more than $100,000 in salary in any single year of their lives!

For instance:

- Dave Ramsey found only 21% of millionaires inherited any money. Of those, just 3% received an inheritance above $1 million.
- The Cato Institute said the notion that "most millionaires inherit their wealth" is a myth. In fact, "70% of wealthy Americans grew up in middle- or lower-class households."
- WealthX discovered that nearly 7 in 10 wealthy people earned their wealth themselves (by starting their own businesses and investing).

While some millionaires get an inheritance, it is important to note that wealth transfer across generations diminishes over time. This means that inherited wealth tends to dissipate over the generations, and the third generation typically depletes the majority of inherited wealth. This reinforces the notion that self-made wealth is the most common type of wealth among today's millionaires.

The evidence directly puts to bed the notion that luck is the primary driver of success, and that's good news! It means success is available to all of us whether we grew up in a rich family or got a big inheritance or not.

We just need to put in the work to get there. And, that's the hard part.

In the end, this is encouraging. It means you don't need to be "lucky" to be successful.

Success doesn't come easy (if it did, we'd all be successful, right?). It takes a lot of hard work. Busting your ass. Saying yes rather than no, as we discussed in the first habit.

Before we continue, let's acknowledge the obvious: yes, luck does exist. After all, we cannot control how we were raised or the color of our skin. We also can't control hereditary illnesses and other physical and mental disabilities that came preinstalled at birth. Clearly, external factors beyond our control exist that affect our success in life, no question about it. But you might be surprised at how much of our lives we have full control over even though we might not want to admit that to ourselves. There are enough rags-to-riches stories in this country to prove that success isn't governed by the aspects of our lives that we can't control. It's the things we can control that make the biggest difference.

Our Choices Compound

Remember when we talked about compound interest in Habit #6? Compounding isn't just a phenomenon with our investments.

Our choices compound. Both positively and negatively. Every choice we make has an effect, and those effects compound over time.

Let's see why.

Take Jimmy. Jimmy had a decent suburban upbringing. He lived in a regular two-story house, took the bus to school, and his mom was home every day after school. But Jimmy made a big mistake when he was a kid. He got involved with the wrong crowd and got busted for auto theft. He went to jail and got a criminal record, and that choice created a domino effect down the line. That choice compounded negatively.

A criminal record means Jimmy can only find minimum-wage jobs. And those minimum wage jobs keep Jimmy from earning enough to invest. Without investing, Jimmy will have a tough time building long-term wealth.

Take Sally. She grew up on the other side of the tracks in low-income housing. She wasn't the popular kid in school but got good enough grades to earn a scholarship to her in-state four-year university. She went to school for accounting, graduated, and got a decent corporate job.

Her job pays enough to start investing. Her investments build. She gets an even better job, gets paid more, and really starts ramping up her investments. She manages to keep her needs reasonable. She drives a 15-year-old car and buys off-brand groceries. By 40, she's a millionaire.

Without knowing the full story, you might consider Sally to be lucky. After all, most people only see the end result of her hard work, not her poor upbringing. And what about Jimmy? Is he unlucky because his criminal record kills his chances of getting a higher-paying job and building wealth?

Here's where it gets interesting.

What if Jimmy goes to a community college to learn more about car repair? He meets an owner of a repair shop in one of his classes who hires Jimmy as a mechanic. Jimmy does a great job, gets promoted to manager, makes friends with a wealthy customer, and they decide to open their own repair shop together.

Same question: Is Jimmy still unlucky or not? Maybe it was "luck" that Jimmy met a wealthy customer who wanted to open a repair shop.

Maybe, but there is another side to that coin: Jimmy put himself into the position to meet that wealthy customer by choosing to go to college and work hard, which helped him meet a business owner who liked his work ethic and gave him a shot.

He chose school. He chose to work hard.

Maybe Jimmy turned negative compounding on its head, reversing the domino effect by attending a community college. If Jimmy's repair shop grows big and he starts making a bunch of money, people will just call Jimmy lucky, won't they? He must have inherited money or had rich parents to help him with the business.

Admittedly, these examples are overly simplified. This is a complicated topic. But, I will say this: Yes, luck exists. Every one of us born to loving parents in the first world and who speak English with access to the Internet is incredibly fortunate.

But then again, there are a lot of fortunate people out there. Some struggle more than others. Life is absolutely harder for some people.

But thankfully, negative compounding can be reversed.

How to Create Your Own Luck

Millionaires know how to create their own luck. We've already talked about many ways millionaires create luck. For instance, saying yes to things that seem uncomfortable puts you in a great position to meet new people, build new skills, and get more opportunities.

Asking for raises at work will help increase your salary. A higher salary will help you stay out of credit card debt, invest for the future, and maybe even retire as a millionaire in your 40s or 50s. Your choice to proactively keep your salary going up has compounded over the years into a million-dollar nest egg that gives you more options in the future, like quitting work early or even taking part-time work so you can travel or spend more time with your family.

Likewise, that fitness routine you start will compound into making you a stronger, healthier, and better-looking version of yourself. Prioritize your workout three days a week for years, and that consistency turns you into a confident and energetic person willing to try new things and make the best of every situation.

Making good choices compounds over time. And those choices are how millionaires create their own luck.

If you still aren't sure how to create your own good luck, don't worry.

Here are 10 ways to turn yourself into a "lucky" person.

Adopt a Positive Mindset

Here's a fact: most people want to associate with positive people. After all, negativity drains our energy and impacts our mood, not in a good way. Positivity will help you to stay focused, motivated, and open to opportunities. If you believe you'll achieve something big, it will probably happen. It won't happen overnight or without hard work. But very often, the first step to achieving big things is believing that you can.

If you're already a positive person, then congrats! You have this one taken care of. But if not, don't fret. Let's talk about how to adopt a positive mindset.

Surround yourself with positivity: The people whom we surround ourselves with make a huge impact on our mood and our mindset. Surround yourself with positive people who inspire you and look on the bright side. Avoid those who are always negative, as that negativity will bring you down.

Practice self-care: As discussed in Habit #2, taking care of yourself physically, mentally, and emotionally is always time well spent. When our needs are addressed, we naturally adopt a more positive outlook. This includes getting enough sleep at night, eating healthy, exercising regularly, and doing things that you enjoy.

Reframe negativity: Negativity is a natural part of life. After all, things will go wrong. We will have stressful days. There's no way to avoid it. But there are ways to manage it. When negative thoughts arise, challenge them and try to reframe them in a more positive light. Instead of saying, "I can't," say, "I'll give it my best shot!" This type of growth mindset puts a positive spin on setbacks and challenges.

Practice gratitude: Take some time to acknowledge all the good that's happening in your life (hint: there is *always* some good). Make a conscious effort to focus on what you are grateful for rather than what you lack. This can help you shift your mindset from one of negativity to one of positivity. For instance, you might not be the fastest runner, but you never have to worry about where your next meal comes from.

Take Calculated Risks

Risks build millionaires. No, I'm not talking about jumping out of perfectly good airplanes with a parachute on your back. That's a very different kind of risk! I mean risks that can make you wealthier or more successful. For instance, there's always risk in investing, though history has shown long-term investing has an exceptionally nice track record of making people rich.

A calculated risk has a better-than-average chance of it paying off. Here are a few ways to determine whether to take a risk.

For instance, let's assume you want to start an ice cream parlor in your town. There's a Dairy Queen already there, but you think a locally owned ice cream shop can succeed.

Understand the reward: Identify the potential risks and rewards of your decision. Make a list of each and weigh them against each other. For instance, if the risk of failure is bigger than the reward of success, it might be too risky.

The reward for starting a successful ice cream shop is clear: it would make you money (assuming you don't eat most of your product!) and perhaps establish you as a positive influence in your town. Your ice cream parlor could also help employ high school kids after school and donate some proceeds to local charities.

What if it fails? Understand the consequences of failure. Can you easily recover if the decision doesn't pan out, or will it significantly impact your life, money, business, or family? Also, what's the worst-case scenario if things go *really* wrong?

If the ice cream parlor fails, you're primarily out of money. Potentially a lot of it. If you took a business loan to buy the ice cream equipment and rent a small shop on Main St., you'd be forced to find a job quickly to repay the loan. You may also feel a little embarrassed with your friends or family because the parlor didn't succeed.

Look for advice: Chances are someone else has already taken the risk. Talk to experts or people who have experience in the area you are considering. Ask them for their input and advice on your decision.

Maybe you have a friend or neighbor who started their own business? Or make friends with the business owner of another shop on Main St. and ask about their challenges. There is also lots of online advice about starting your own local business.

Make a plan: Rather than winging it, make a plan and decide how you will move forward with the calculated risk. Consider any contingencies or potential roadblocks that may arise, and have a plan for how you will handle them.

Your ice cream parlor's business plan might look something like this:

Sally's Ice Cream Parlor will offer a variety of high-quality ice cream flavors and toppings in a welcoming and family-friendly atmosphere. We will focus on providing exceptional customer service and a unique experience for our customers, including free samples and regular discounts on holidays and during the annual Main St. Fair. Our goal is to become a local favorite for ice cream lovers.

The ice cream industry has been growing steadily in recent years, and there is a growing demand for high-quality, artisanal ice cream from locally owned store owners. Our audience includes children, young adults, and tourists. We will be in a busy area with high foot traffic, making us easily accessible to our target market. We will be open from 11 a.m. to 8 p.m. with extended closing hours of 10 p.m. during the summer.

Estimated start-up costs will be around $120,000, which includes equipment, rent, inventory, and employee salaries. Our projected revenue for the first year is $250,000, with a net profit of $50,000. We will reinvest 80% of our profits into marketing and expanding our product line.

Monitor your progress: Keep an eye on the results of your decision. The sooner you spot potential roadblocks, the easier it will be to adjust and avoid a larger failure.

Keeping a close eye on your ice cream parlor's financials will ensure your new business does well. For instance, if your customers come in later than usual, you might consider extending your closing time to 11 p.m. during summer. Or if ice cream storage costs are higher than anticipated, you may need to raise prices or cut back on employee hours to compensate for that additional cost.

Be Proactive

Millionaires don't wait for things to happen to them. Instead, they make things happen, and they do this by being proactive in every facet of their lives. Being proactive puts you squarely in the driver's seat, allowing you to control your career and life fully.

Believe it or not, being proactive is a skill that needs to be practiced. To many of us (me included), taking the initiative can seem daunting or scary, but the more we do it, the easier it gets.

When you're proactive, you're better able to identify potential problems and come up with solutions before they become serious. This can help you develop stronger problem-solving skills and become more resilient in facing challenges. And believe me, employers are quick to promote those who can identify problems before they happen and propose solutions.

For instance, recognizing that you are underpaid and asking for a raise (or switching jobs) is a good example of being proactive rather than hoping that your salary eventually catches up. We discussed both of these tactics in Habit #3, and it's something millionaires do regularly to ensure their salary keeps up with inflation.

Here are a few other examples of being proactive (hint: we talk a lot about these examples elsewhere in the book—these are habits of millionaires!):

Regular exercise: Being fit and healthy improves energy and confidence. Make exercise a part of your everyday routine, not just something you do if you have time.

Writing a daily to-do list: Writing a to-do list every day (or the night before) gives you marching orders from when you wake up and can start your day off right.

Constant mental check-ins: Do you feel happy and productive? Is your relationship going well? Is your career right for you? Always check in with yourself, and be honest!

Being the first one in the office: I was always one of the first every day, which made a big difference. I got more done by 10 a.m. than most did the entire day.

Volunteering for extra responsibilities: Asking for more work is a great way to get raises and promotions. It means you're serious, productive, and engaged. That's money!

Asking questions rather than assuming: Successful people ask for help when needed rather than plowing through unclear assignments and then having to do them over.

Be Open-minded

At one point in my life, I firmly believed that to be a good manager, you had to be a hard ass. Like a drill sergeant. Your staff had to be just a little bit afraid of you. It was your way or the highway.

Luckily, I outgrew that incredibly stupid belief because I was open-minded enough to observe that some of the best managers I ever worked for were personable and smiled a lot. They listened to me and valued my input and suggestions. And these are the types of people I always wanted to work for. I don't need a drill sergeant on my case daily. Who wants that?

Being open-minded means accepting the fact that your beliefs, perceptions, and experiences may not tell the whole story in life. After all, reality is very fluid. What works for one person may not work for another. What motivates someone who works extra hard in the office may not be the same thing that motivates another.

For instance, I was always motivated by money. The harder I worked, the better position I was in to get raises and promotions, and that helped me achieve my goal of becoming a millionaire. But I also worked with those who preferred extra vacation time, skipped out early on Fridays, or had better health benefits. Everybody's motivations are different.

And that's okay. After all, how boring would the world be if we all wanted the exact same thing? Being different is good. And the more open we are to each other's differences, the more effective we will be. And as a result, the richer we will become.

What are the characteristics of open-minded people?

- They don't always have to be right.
- They are empathetic with how other people feel.
- They embrace having their own opinions challenged.
- They want to hear thoughts and feedback from others.
- They understand their experiences don't tell the whole story.

Now, I'm not telling you to gather your coworkers or friends around a campfire, hold hands, and sing "Kumbaya" after telling each other intimate and creepy stories about yourselves. Certainly not, because that's pretty weird.

I am saying being open-minded puts you in a position of respect and loyalty. After all, nobody respects drill sergeants in the workplace. But managers who care about their staff and actively seek their opinions are respected. People would do anything for them.

Visualize Your Success

Have you ever said this to yourself with something you really want: "I want to drive that car so bad, I can practically feel it!"

Believe it or not, that type of visualization is a millionaire habit. You can see yourself driving that car. The wind in your hair. The smooth hum of the engine and the throaty exhaust note. The back-against-the-seat torque as you accelerate. You get the idea. You want something so bad that you can visualize yourself being there.

To visualize your success, you need two things in place:

1. Know Your Definition of Success

Success means something different for everyone. My definition of success was quitting my job and traveling the country with my wife and two dogs. But it might (and probably will!) look very different for you.

What is your definition of success? Or, in other words, what needs to happen for you to say, "I've made it finally"? This is a difficult question for most people to answer, so if you don't have an answer right now, that's okay. You don't need to have one this instant. However, consider this question and decide what success means to you.

For example, maybe success means starting your own business that earns multiple six figures per year. Or perhaps you want to quit working to stay home and be there when your kids get home from school. Maybe success means earning enough money to quit your job, move to Fiji, and open a beach-side coffee shop.

2. Understand How It Will Make You Feel

Why is your definition of success what it is? How will it make you feel once you've achieved it? Get to the bottom of what motivates you in life.

For my wife and me, our motivation was rooted in freedom. The freedom to travel and go anywhere we want, at a moment's notice, without having to worry about money. The feeling of complete and utter autonomy over every nook and cranny of our lives motivated us to work hard, rapidly acquire as much wealth as possible, and then quit our jobs to pursue our next life of travel and adventure.

If you want to start your own business, why? Why do you want to move to Fiji? Why do you want to get rich? Again, this question is tough for many to answer, but the answer will help connect your definition of success with the underlying reason behind it. Knowing the why behind your success will help keep you motivated and focused on making it happen. Close your eyes and visualize yourself exactly where you want to be.

Where are you? Are you on the beach? Are you in a bustling city? Maybe out in the country on acres of land without another person for miles. Or maybe you're traveling by backpack in a land far, far away.

Then, ask yourself a simple question: Why are you happy?

Work Hard

There's nothing quite like hard work that makes cash appear in your wallet, almost like magic. You'll hear people talk about hacks and strategies to work less and still make money, but hard work is the age-old strategy that's never fallen out of style for millionaires. It still works. And it always will.

Working hard is how you make money. It puts you in a position to get the promotions you want and the raises you deserve. But working hard has a variety of benefits outside of just making money.

Hard work helps you to:

Achieve your goals: Hard work is a prerequisite for achieving your goals. Whether getting a job promotion, starting a business, or learning a new skill, working hard will help you progress toward your desired outcome.

Build self-discipline: Working hard helps you develop self-discipline, an essential trait for success in any area of life. Self-discipline helps you stay focused, motivated, and committed to your goals.

Improve your skills: Hard work allows you to practice and develop your skills, which can lead to mastery and expertise in any field. This can help you become more valuable to employers or customers and drastically increase your earning potential.

Boost your confidence: Completing difficult tasks through hard work can help boost your confidence and self-esteem for the next task. This, in turn, can help you tackle new challenges with greater ease and optimism. Hard work snowballs your confidence.

Gain respect: Hard work is often recognized and respected by others. People tend to admire and appreciate your dedication and perseverance when you put in the effort and achieve results. People will notice even though they may not say anything to you.

Feel fulfilled: Working hard will give you a sense of satisfaction and fulfillment, knowing that you've tried to achieve your goals. This can contribute to your overall happiness and well-being. Face it: we feel better after we work hard to finish a task.

Build a high-quality Network

You've probably heard the phrase "Your network is your net worth." It means that the value of the relationships you've built with others, including personal and professional contacts, is extremely important to your overall success and financial well-being.

In other words, the people you know and the connections you make are as valuable as money in the bank. Building and maintaining a strong network leads to new opportunities, business partnerships, and other valuable connections that can help you achieve your goals and increase your success.

Not to name-drop here, but Harvard Social Psychologist Dr. David McClelland happens to agree. He said the people you habitually associate with determine as much as 95 percent of your success or failure in life. Millionaires know how true that statement is.

If you associate with people who are avid gym-goers and focus on their health, chances are you will too. On the other hand, if you hang out with people who smoke or get drunk every chance they get, then again, you'll likely wind up stumbling down that same path.

When I talk about leveling up the people you hang around, the most common question I get is this: "How do I find these people?"

Good question. Believe it or not, many of these people are already in our lives, though we may not realize it. We have our immediate group of friends and it's far too easy to ignore everyone else. You might be surprised at the networking opportunities that are right in front of you but you haven't taken the time to notice (I'm guilty of this!).

Here are a few other ideas to help you build a high-quality network:

Attend networking events: Attend industry events, seminars, and conferences. These events are a great way to meet new people in your field, learn from experts and industry leaders, and stay up-to-date on the latest trends and news.

Join professional associations: Joining professional associations in your industry is a great way to meet like-minded people, expand your knowledge and skills, and build relationships with others who share your interests.

Use social media: Social media platforms such as LinkedIn, Twitter, and Instagram are great tools for connecting with others in your field. I spend a lot of time on Twitter, and it's been amazing the people I've met on that platform. I've tweeted with billionaire and Dallas Mavericks owner Mark Cuban, professional athletes, successful business owners, and countless others I would probably never have met in real life.

Volunteer or join clubs: Volunteer for charitable organizations or join clubs that align with your interests. This can be a great way to meet new people, build relationships, and contribute to your community. More on volunteering later in this chapter.

Build relationships: Building strong relationships takes time and effort. Keep in touch with people in your network, send a quick message or email to catch up, and offer to help others whenever possible. I always like to reach out to someone in my network once a month to catch up on their work and see how I can help them.

Ditch Your Comfort Zone

Comfort zones are where dreams go to die. That's a tough statement, but think about what a comfort zone is and why it won't help you achieve your goals.

Achieving goals is hard work. It's not comfortable. Being successful often means doing things that make us uncomfortable, such as giving presentations in front of groups of people or putting in 50 hours of overtime in a month to finish a big project. Success isn't always comfortable, and that's okay. In fact, that's good. Overcoming challenges makes us stronger people. Most of us don't accomplish amazing things from our comfort zones.

Here are a few ways to help you ditch your comfort zone:

Try new things: Whether trying a new hobby or learning a new skill, trying something new can be a great way to challenge yourself and step out of your comfort zone. Choose an activity you've always been interested in but never tried before, and commit to it. For instance, want to start a garden? This weekend, do it! Build that planter box. Get your hands into the soil.

Travel somewhere new: Exploring a new place can be an excellent way to broaden your horizons and experience new things. I'm always amazed at people who have never left their home state, because there is so much of the country to see. Consider traveling somewhere you've never been before, whether it's a different country or just a different town nearby. Traveling to other countries is also an excellent way to learn about other people's lives.

Take on a new challenge: Challenge yourself by taking on a new project or task that you've never done before. It could be something as simple as learning a new recipe or as challenging as running a marathon. Give yourself a goal and time to complete it. Challenges can be fun, especially if they are achievable.

Meet new people: Meeting new people and socializing can be a great way to step out of your comfort zone. Attend a social event or join a new group or club to meet new people and expand your social circle. I joined a grotto club in my hometown several years ago and found it to be a very rewarding experience, and I'm still friends with many of those I met in the grotto club to this day.

Say yes to new opportunities: We've talked at length about this one, but it is important enough to mention it again. When new opportunities arise, say yes, even if it scares you. It could be a job opportunity, a new adventure, or an invitation to try something new.

Face your fears: Identify your fears and work toward overcoming them. Whether it's public speaking, heights, or spiders, facing your fears can be a significant step toward stepping out of your comfort zone. Often, conquering our fears help us to understand that there's nothing to be afraid of.

Change your routine: Mix up your daily routine by trying new things or doing things differently. This could include taking a different route to work, trying a new breakfast food, or changing your workout routine. Heck, it might also mean switching jobs or moving to another city. I changed jobs every three to four years because I loved changing my routine. That habit kept my skills improving and my salary going up.

Volunteer

Volunteering for a cause we care about is something a lot of millionaires do. In fact, nearly three-quarters (72%) of millionaires said they volunteer at least five hours a month at local nonprofits.[1] Volunteering is not only a great way to help your local community, but it's also an effective way to meet more people and continually expand your network of friends and associates.

Want to volunteer but not sure where to start? Here are a few ideas:

Work at an animal shelter: Help out at an animal shelter by walking dogs, cleaning cages, serving meals, or helping with administrative tasks.

Tutor or mentor students: Give your time at a local school or community center to tutor or mentor children who need extra help with their studies.

Clean up your community: Join a local clean-up effort to help remove litter and debris from streets, parks, and other public spaces. Hint: most cities need this!

Volunteer at a local hospital or nursing home: Help out at a hospital or nursing home by spending time with patients, reading to them, or helping with creative activities.

Serve meals at a soup kitchen or food bank: Serve meals at a soup kitchen or food bank, or volunteer to sort and package donated food items.

There are so many different ways to donate your time and give back. If you're short on time, consider donating money instead of your time to charities such as The American Red Cross, The Salvation Army, Habitat for Humanity, St. Jude Children's Hospital, Doctors Without Borders, or the Make-A-Wish Foundation.

Take Action: How to Change Your Luck

Put yourself out there. There is only one step to changing your own luck, and that's getting off the couch and start taking action. Use some of the examples in this chapter to adopt a "luckier" lifestyle.

One of my favorite techniques is building relationships. This was never easy for me (I'm a natural introvert), but I found that the more people I met, the more opportunities I had. By meeting new people and expanding your network, you put yourself into a position to get more opportunities just by virtue of being there.

It's amazing how just being there can drastically improve your luck.

Note

1. Corley, T. "10 Common Millionaire Habits." Acorns (2022). https://www.acorns.com/learn/earning/common-millionaire-habits/.

Habit #9

Millionaires Control Their Spending

Despite what you might think, millionaires don't spend like drunken sailors. In fact, the majority of millionaires are millionaires because they've combined three primary wealth-building principles:

1. Maximizing income;
2. Consistent investing;
3. Controlling expenses.

We've already discussed numbers 1 and 2 at length. This chapter is about the third one—the one that isn't as fun to talk about but is critically important. Let's talk about controlling your expenses without making your life feel like a sacrifice.

For example, money gurus tell you your morning cup-o-Joe is destroying your wealth, but I couldn't disagree more. If that morning coffee gets you going, then ignore what the "experts" tell you, and just buy the damn coffee. Yes, it's okay.

Millionaires control their expenses not by ruthlessly slashing the things that mean the most to them to save a buck. On the contrary, I fully support spending generously on the things that are important to you and cutting back on everything else. After all, we'll be far more likely to control our spending habits if we allow ourselves to splurge a bit.

This isn't about cutting the stuff we love. This chapter is about cutting the stuff we don't.

Let's begin by discussing something that 99 percent of people get wrong.

Your Income Doesn't Equal Your Wealth

Let's say you're bringing home $250,000 a year. Cool, right? You're rich. You have enough money to spend on just about anything you want. Those season tickets? No problem. A lake house? Yep. The latest iPhone every year? Sign me up!

It isn't just sports stars who fall victim to the high-income, high-spending trap. Chances are your neighbor, or your neighbor's neighbor, is overspending their means because they believe they can afford it.

I've worked with a lot of people just like this. They earned a big salary and proceeded to spend the majority of it on cars, vacation homes, and all the latest gadgets. As a result, they were deathly afraid of losing their jobs because their lifestyles required them not just to work but to work a stressful, high-paying job to pay for their expenses.

Let's do the math. If that $250,000/year earning spends $200,000 a year, they only have $50,000 a year to save and invest. While $50,000 is better than nothing, it's only a fraction of their yearly income, putting them into a financially compromising situation. They may be only one job loss or unexpected medical emergency away from either losing everything they have or going deep into debt to pay for it.

Here are two statements that millionaires understand:

Earning a high salary doesn't mean you're rich.
Just because you have enough money doesn't mean you can afford it.

Earning a big salary increases your chances of becoming rich if you're smart with managing your money. However, building wealth isn't automatic just because your salary is high. You need to be thoughtful and meticulous about the things you spend money on. High salaries are great, but they are also just the beginning.

The Five-step Framework to Control Your Spending

Still reading? Good, because this is where things start to fall into place. For most people, spending control isn't easy.

Step 1: Identify All Your Expenses

I cannot stress this enough: It's impossible to control your spending habits if you're unclear about where your money is going. A lot of people are in this boat. I was too, before I decided to prioritize financial freedom. I won't lie, this step kinda sucks. But it's also a key element in improving how you spend your money.

Think of it like learning to ride a bike. We need to fall and scrape our knees a few times before we ride comfortably. It's a step none of us likes, but it's necessary.

Here's what you need to do.

First, go through your bank and credit card statements for at least the past three months (see, I told you this was going to suck—but again, it's necessary, and you'll only need to do this once!). Categorize every single expense. This will help you pinpoint areas of your spending that are too much, too little, or areas you did no know existed. The idea is to add up exactly how you spend your money today per month.

Common spending categories include:

- Rent or mortgage;
- Transportation (bus fees, gas);
- Food (groceries, coffee);
- Utilities (electric, gas);
- Restaurants;

- Savings;
- Insurance (car, health);
- Personal care (haircuts, massages);
- Entertainment (movies, sports, concerts);
- Debt repayment.

With every single line item, tally that expense in the appropriate category. Do this for one month, and then add each category to determine how much you spent in that category. Then, move on to the second month. Then the third.

If you aren't good at math, don't worry. Use a spreadsheet. Put each category across the top. Each subsequent row will represent a charge on your credit card or bank statement.

Let's take a look at an example:

Rent	Food	Restaurants	Transportation	Entertainment
850				
	54.23			
		78.97		
			35.22	
	84.66			
				15.23
				94.32
	133.40			
850	**272.29**	**78.97**	**35.22**	**109.55**

This is a very simple example, but it demonstrates how to track and categorize each expense (your spreadsheet will likely be considerably longer). At the bottom, each expense is totaled. And presto! You know exactly how much money you spend each month in each category. Repeat this process for each month so you have a total for each category per month.

Remember that your spending categories might need to be more detailed than those in the example. For instance, you might want to track how much you spend on clothes for each child rather than a lump sum for the entire family (in fact, I highly recommend getting a little more detailed whenever you can).

Here's what that might look like in your spreadsheet:

Clothing – Mom	Clothing – Dad	Clothing – Rebecca	Clothing – Nathan

Armed with this information, you'll also be able to determine what percentage of your income you're spending and where.

According to the popular 50/30/20 rule, you should spend 50 percent of your income on your basic living expenses (needs) for survival, including your rent or mortgage, cars, insurance, food, minimum debt payments, and so forth. Note: restaurant spending isn't included in this. While you need food, you don't have to eat at Chipotle to live, do you? In a previous life, I probably would have said "yes" to this question!

Thirty percent of your income can be spent on wants. These items include a new watch, sports tickets, vacations, new cell phones, morning coffee, and so forth. Anything that isn't absolutely critical but you want anyway is included here. This is your *fun* spending.

Lastly, 20 percent is for saving and investing. This includes building an emergency fund, contributing toward your employer-sponsored 401(k), IRAs, and anything else that's related to saving money or investing in assets. Note that this can also include repaying debts beyond your minimum payment (because your minimum payment is required).

This information is extremely useful, as we will discuss in Step 2.

Step 2: Decide on Expenses to Cut or Reduce

Now that you know where all your money is going every month, it's time to make some serious decisions. Don't be surprised if you're shocked by how much money you spend in some categories. When I went through this process, my restaurant spending nearly sent me running for the hills. I was spending way more to eat out than

I thought I was. For me, restaurant spending was the first thing I cut back on.

Your job is to look honestly at how much you're spending each month and decide where you can reduce your spending. Make this a family decision if you can. At the very least, confirm with your spouse to ensure everyone is on the same page.

This isn't the time to be judgmental. If you're spending $1,000 on restaurants monthly, don't get angry with yourself (or someone else). Instead, decide how much you can cut back. There is no need to eliminate going out to eat. Instead, just cook at home a few extra nights a week. The goal here is to reduce, not to eliminate.

Let's look at a couple of examples of how this might work.

Example 1: You spent $500 on clothes for your daughter last month, which seems high. But you didn't spend a dime on her clothes over the two previous months. This is an example of a one-time expense that doesn't accurately reflect your month-to-month spending. In this case, the best way to track monthly clothes spending for your daughter is to add up your daughter's clothes spending for an entire year and then average that spending across all 12 months.

For instance, if you spend $600 a year on clothes for your daughter, the average monthly spend is $50 (600/12). This will make it easier to determine if $50 a month is too much or just about right.

Example 2: Gas for the car is setting you back over $400 a month (the average American spends around $200 on gas for their car). You take some time to think about how much your family uses the car and quickly realize that you're driving to the grocery store nearly daily to pick up one or two items for dinner. To reduce gas spending, you make detailed grocery lists to buy everything you need at once rather than forgetting something and running back out when needed.

Example 3: Your heating costs are extremely high in the winter. It's natural to spend more during the winter months to heat your home, but it also shouldn't break the bank. To reduce costs, you decide to reseal your windows, ensure all outside doors are regularly closed, and turn down the heat at night to 62 and down to

40 when you take that Christmas vacation to Grandma's. You also decide to upgrade your home's ducting to improve airflow efficiency, which is an upfront cost but saves you money month after month, both in the winter and the summer.

Remember—and I cannot stress this enough—this isn't the time to get angry or judgmental. Pinpointing areas of your life where you are overspending is the point of this exercise. Chances are you will find categories of overspending. That's good!

Identifying these areas is the only way to start cutting back.

Step 3: Create a Spending Plan

Creating a monthly spending plan is a great way to visualize how much money you can spend in each monthly category. If you combine a monthly spending plan with the Pay Yourself First philosophy discussed in Habit #4, you can set yourself up to build drastically more wealth than just winging it every month.

As we learned in Habit #4, Pay Yourself First works on the assumption that we fully fund our savings and investments and pay our bills first. The beauty is after these spending categories are funded, the rest of our money is ours to spend at will, no judgment.

Your spending plan will include three primary types of spending (and let's match up each type with how they fit into the 50/30/20 spending guideline). Notice that the spending categories you mapped out earlier all fit somewhere inside these three major types of monthly spending:

- **Required to live (50%):** Expenses that are required, such as your mortgage or rent, minimum debt payments, home utilities, groceries, etc. These expenses always come first because you must feed your family, and missing payments incur fees and penalties. To reduce these expenses, decide what is most important as a family, and then cut the rest.
- **Investing and saving (20%):** As discussed in Habit #6, investing is how people become millionaires. Typical investments include employee-sponsored 401(k)s and Roth IRAs plans,

brokerage accounts, stocks, bonds, ETFs, REITs, and crypto-currencies. Savings goals include vacations, your child's college education, a down payment for a house, a new boat, etc. This also includes saving a three- to six-month emergency fund, which is critical to avoid going into credit card debt to fund costly unexpected expenses.

- **No-judgment spending (30%):** Everything else such as cable TV, Starbucks, season tickets to the Lakers, weekly ice cream parlor visits with the kids, restaurants, mani-pedis, etc. This is the fun type of spending!

If you adopt the Pay Yourself First method (by now, you should know that I highly endorse that method!), your required expenses, savings, and investing goals are taken care of first. Remember that in Step 2, you decided on areas to cut spending back. It's critical that you continue to track your spending to ensure that you're not accidentally overspending (more on this in Step 4). But for now, let's assume that your bills, investments, and savings goals have all been fully funded.

Once the bills, savings, and investments are out of the way, our "No-judgment" spending (the fun stuff!) is where we have some decisions to make. As we learned in Step 1 of this process, no-judgment spending can take up to about 30 percent of your salary.

Step 4: Track Your Expenses

By now, you have the foundation in place. You know how much you're spending. And most importantly, you have a good idea of where your money is going. This alone puts you ahead of about 90 percent of people. So congratulations!

Your work isn't done yet (although the toughest part is!). Unfortunately, this isn't one of those "set it and forget it" investing strategies I discussed in this book. This is one of those areas where an active approach beats a passive one every time.

To keep on your spending plan, you need to keep track of your monthly expenses to ensure you're not going over. Every month, add up every expense from every spending category from Step 1. If you're going over, cut back. Or if you find that you need to spend more in a particular category, there's nothing wrong with increasing your spending plan to allow for that increase. However, be honest with yourself and make sure any additional spending truly is required and not just desired.

If that feels like a chore, don't worry. Luckily, many tools can help you track your spending so you aren't diving through your statements and manually adding up all those beautiful numbers. Not all of these tools are free, but I've found that the spending visibility you get more than pays for the monthly cost.

A couple of tools I like:

Mint: One of the most popular budgeting apps around, Mint (free!) helps track your month-to-month spending and helps visualize your cash flow (money in vs. money out). Mint is from Intuit, a well-established financial services company.

You Need A Budget: Clean and easy to use, this tool is a good option for tracking your spending every month. Connect the app to your financial institutions (like your banks and credit cards), and it'll do the rest. The app also helps track your savings goals (e.g. that vacation to Tahiti, a new Murphy bed). Note this tool is not free.

Note: Another benefit of expense tracking is catching fraudulent or incorrect credit card or bank statement charges. Most credit cards give customers 60 days to dispute charges, and expense tracking will ensure you catch and correct any fraud or mistakes on your bill before it's too late.

Step 5: Set Financial Goals

The last step (although this can happen at any time) is to set your financial goals, so you have a reason to save money. For most people, just saving "for retirement" isn't enough of a goal. The best goals are concrete and achievable.

For instance, if you don't have an emergency fund, that should be your first financial goal. Priority number one! Get that rainy day fund set up. Use the power of automation to help you funnel money to a separate savings account to start building your emergency fund.

If you're in debt (especially high-interest credit card debt), your goal might be to become debt-free, minus the mortgage if you have one). I talk about exactly how to achieve this goal in Habit #10.

But let's say you have your financial house in order. No debts. A healthy three-plus month emergency fund. What other financial goals might you have?

Here are a few examples:

- $500,000 net worth by 45;
- A down payment on a new house;
- Funding your child's college education;
- That vacation to the Bahamas with the family;
- Quit your nine-to-five job by 50 to start that gardening business.

Giving yourself a reason to save will make it far more likely that you will stick with your new spending plan. These financial goals are those reasons.

The Difference between Cheap and Frugal

This chapter is all about saving money. But that doesn't mean you're always buying the least expensive thing. In fact, buying the cheapest product often costs you more money in the long run. This is the difference between cheap and frugal.

You want to be frugal. Being cheap isn't necessary.

To illustrate the difference, let's take a look at an example.

Suppose you're shopping for a new pair of shoes. You need your shoes to last, as you're on your feet often during the day. You like your current pair, and they've lasted a couple of years, but they also cost $150. Instead of plunking down that much money again, you pick up a cheaper pair for only $85.

At the time of the purchase, you feel good. After all, you just "saved" $65 by choosing the less expensive pair of shoes. However, the downside is that pair of shoes only lasted a year before the sole began tearing away from the rest of the shoe.

You decide to bite the bullet and get that $150 pair of shoes again, knowing that getting the cheaper pair that wore out quicker was the more expensive choice. In the end, you spent more.

Here's another example. You're planning a vacation with some friends and choose to book the cheapest accommodation available without considering the location, amenities, or cleanliness. You insist on splitting every expense down to the last penny, including meals, transportation, and activities. You constantly look for ways to avoid spending money, even if it means inconveniencing yourself or your friends. You opt for the cheapest and most basic options in every aspect, compromising comfort and enjoyment of your vacation time. This is cheap.

A frugal person might research and compare different accommodation options, considering factors such as location, safety, amenities, and reviews. You look for deals, discounts, or loyalty programs to get the best value for your money. You discuss with your friends to set a budget and agree to share costs fairly. You plan your meals strategically, opting for affordable yet delicious local eateries or even preparing some meals yourself. You prioritize experiences that are worth the expense and find free or low-cost activities and attractions in the area.

Being cheap means focusing solely on spending the least money possible, even for an inferior product or service, sacrificing comfort, quality, and enjoyment. Being frugal, you understand that buying a higher-quality product will likely save you money in the long run and make whatever you're buying much more enjoyable, which is the point of buying it in the first place, right?

There is no need to be cheap and deprive yourself of what you enjoy.

However, there are ways to have fun without spending much money. Into museums? Some have promotions for free or low-cost entrance fees every so often. Instead of paying hundreds of dollars for a concert ticket, consider checking out that free concert at your local park or amphitheater. You might be surprised at how much entertainment is available for free (or low cost), especially if you're willing to avoid going on holidays or weekends when promotions and specials are less common.

The 72-hour Rule

Tell me if this sounds familiar: You want something. Say, a new wireless charger for your phone, a big-screen television, or a new kitchen appliance. You pull up Amazon, find what you want, and buy the sucker with the click of a button. Boom, done.

Then it ends up sitting in the box for a while because you don't really need it yet, or at all. Or you use it once, and then it sits in your closet or garage.

This happens to many of us, and Amazon knows it. Amazon makes it so darn easy to buy something we think we want without giving it a second thought. It's just too easy to spend money. We want something. We buy it.

An easy way to rein in your online spending is to adopt the 72-hour rule.

Instead of straight-up buying something that you want, just add it to your shopping cart. Then after about three days (or 72 hours), return to it and make sure you still want it. If you do, then it might be worth the money. But you might be surprised at how often we'll change our minds about something or figure out we don't need it after all.

For most of us, this is an easy change. It just requires us to wait a few more days before buying the things we think we need.

Take Action: Here's What You Need to Do

Step 1: Start with the 5-Step framework. Buckle down and learn where your money goes monthly because every subsequent step stems from this knowledge. No judgments. No arguments. To use a legal term, this is the "discovery" phase. You're accumulating evidence that you will use to start making better decisions with your money.

Step 2: Implement the 72-hour rule. Before making any more online purchases, commit to keeping those items in your cart for 72 hours before making the purchase. If you still want those items after three days, buy them.

Step 3: Stick with it. The key to improving your spending is sticking with it. Like a new diet, you won't see any real, earth-shattering (in a good way!) changes to your financial health if you try it for a month, then ditch it altogether, and go back to spending as you always had. Unfortunately, a lot of people do this.

One of the best ways to stick with it is by getting a spouse on board with the process. Having another person involved provides accountability.

"Honey, do you really think we should be buying this? It's not in the budget."

I know it sounds annoying, but it's a critical part of keeping yourselves honest as you implement a brand-new way of spending money.

Habit #10

Millionaires Stay Out of [Bad] Debt

Debts are like throwing sand straight into your car's gas tank. Your car will run for a couple of miles, but there's no way you're making the entire 10-mile trip to pick up your kids from soccer practice.

Let me tell you a story.

Once upon a time, there was a guy named Sam. Sam was a hardworking person with a steady job and enjoyed his life. One day, Sam wanted to buy a new car. A Cadillac, of course, because Sam felt he deserved that car. However, Sam didn't have enough cash to pay for it, so he decided to take out a loan to buy the car.

No big deal, right? Many people have auto loans, so this shouldn't be a problem for Sam.

At first, Sam felt pretty good about it. He liked the thought of driving around in a brand-new Cadillac. And because he could afford the monthly payments, he felt secure in buying an expensive car.

But over time, things started to change.

Sam's other expenses started accumulating, and he realized he struggled to pay his bills. He liked the flexibility of spending money on things he wanted without actually having the money in cash. His auto loan whetted his appetite, and he started spending more and more on credit cards. He paid the minimum on each card and let the rest ride month after month.

In the back of his mind, he knew that interest was accruing, but he didn't care. He was living well, working hard, and having fun.

Soon, Sam lived paycheck to paycheck, barely making ends meet. His credit score started to drop, and he began to receive calls from debt collectors. The stress of his financial situation began to affect his relationships and health.

Sam realized that the debt he had taken on for his car and credit cards had become a burden that he couldn't shake off. He regretted taking out the loan and wished he had saved up for a less expensive car. Now, he was stuck with a Cadillac that he couldn't really afford, and his financial future was uncertain.

The lesson of Sam's story is that debt can quickly become a trap if you're not careful.

Taking out loans or using credit cards can seem like an easy solution to get what you want now, but it can come at a high cost later on. It's important to be mindful of your spending and avoid taking on more debt than you can repay.

Worse, debts cause more than just money trouble. It also causes relationship friction. An Ally study found that money was the primary cause of relationship stress 36% of the time.[1] Debt causes relationship struggles.

The Two Types of Debt

Believe it or not, good debts exist. Yes, that's right! But that doesn't mean that the debt you have right now is good.

The difference between good and bad debt is whether the debt is an investment in your future or a liability that will cost you money. Good debt can help you reach your financial goals faster, such as owning a home, paying for school, or starting a business.

Bad debt is debt that does not have any long-term benefits and can actually hurt your financial situation.

Most consumer debts (the types of debt you and I have) are not good.

Bad debts are high-interest debts that destroy our wealth-building potential. Credit card debt is the best example. Payday loans are another example of a bad debt to avoid at all costs (pun intended!). Other examples of bad debt include title loans, which use your car title as collateral, and store credit cards, which often have high-interest rates and fees.

Okay, so what are good debts?

Good debts are debts on appreciating assets. In other words, it's probably a good debt if you're borrowing money to build or buy something that can make you more (and often, substantially more) than you borrowed.

A few examples of good debt include:

Student loans: Borrowing money to invest in education and skills can lead to higher income and better job prospects from those skills, making it a worthwhile investment. The higher the income potential of your chosen career field, the more likely it is that the student loans will turn into good debt. For instance, a degree in medieval puppetry probably isn't worth the student debt, as most companies aren't looking for puppet masters. But accounting, computer science, electrical engineering, and nursing? Many degree programs have a proven track record of high salaries and job security. Student loans are best used in preparation for work in high-paying career fields.

Mortgages: Taking out a mortgage to purchase a home can be a good investment as property values typically appreciate over time, creating equity that can be used to build wealth. However, remember that we often make less money on our homes due to costs associated with their upkeep.

Small business loans: Borrowing money to start or grow a small business can increase revenue and profits, creating a positive return on investment.

Real estate investments: Borrowing money to invest in real estate properties that generate rental income (in other words, being a landlord for properties you own) can be a good source of passive income, allowing you to build wealth over time.

These are considered good debts because of the potential to make more money than you borrowed. However, many Americans hold bad debt, and these are the debts you need to avoid if you want to become a millionaire.

What are bad debts? Here are several examples:

Credit cards: Carrying a balance month-to-month on your credit cards is the most common type of bad debt. The high-interest rate will accumulate and make it difficult to pay off the balance, which can lead to a crippling cycle of debt. A GoBankingRates survey found that 30% of Americans have between $1,001 and $5,000 of credit card debt.[2] That isn't good!

To illustrate just how terrible credit card debts can be, let's use an example. Remember our discussion of compound interest and how amazing it is when we make it work for us by investing? Credit card debt turns that 180 degrees on its head. That very same compound interest is working against us this time.

Suppose you have a credit card balance of $1,000 with an annual interest rate of 20%. If you only make the minimum monthly payment of $25, your interest will accrue on the remaining balance after each payment.

In the first month, your interest will be calculated based on the $1,000 balance, which is $16.67 ($1,000 × 20% / 12). After you make your minimum payment of $25, your balance will be $991.67 ($1,000 − $25 + $16.67).

In the second month, your interest will be calculated based on the new balance of $991.67, which is $16.53 ($991.67 × 20% / 12). After you make your minimum payment of $25, your balance will be $983.20 ($991.67 − $25 + $16.53).

This process will continue each month, with your interest compounding on the remaining balance after each payment. As you can see, the interest charges add up quickly, and it can take a long time to pay off your debt if you only make minimum payments.

How long? You might want to sit down for this (wait, are you reading this book standing up?). Making only a minimum payment of $25 on a $1,000 credit card debt at 20% interest will take you five and a half years to pay it off. Worse, you would have paid $662 in interest during that period, turning that $1,000 debt into $1,662.

And this assumes no additional charges are made to that credit card.

What if you paid $50 a month, double the minimum payment? You'd be wrong if you think your interest paid and the number of years it would take to pay it off is cut in half. It's better than that. It would take you over two years to pay off that $1,000 debt making $50 monthly payments. And you would only pay $227 in interest. Paying double the minimum makes a significant difference!

Any way you slice it, you end up paying substantially more for everything you buy due to the interest that credit card companies charge. That's why paying more than the minimum each month is important to avoid getting trapped in a cycle of debt.

The best way to use credit cards is to pay off the entire balance each month, which means you're paying $0 in credit card debt.

Payday loans: Payday loans are often seen as a quick solution to financial problems, but they can quickly become bad debts due to their high-interest rates, fees, and tight repayment deadlines.

Payday loans are typically used to cover emergency expenses or unexpected bills (for those who don't have an emergency fund!). These loans are usually for small amounts, ranging from a few hundred to a few thousand dollars, and are typically due on the borrower's next payday. Essentially, you are borrowing money against your next paycheck.

Getting a payday loan typically involves the following steps:

- **An application:** The borrower provides personal, employment, and banking information to the payday lender.
- **Lender performs verifications:** The lender may ask for additional documentation or contact the borrower's employer to verify employment and income.
- **Lender approves the loan:** If the lender determines that the borrower is eligible for a payday loan, they will approve the loan and provide the borrower with the loan terms, including the interest rate and fees.

- **Borrower receives the funds:** If the borrower agrees to the loan terms, the lender will provide the funds in cash or by depositing the money into the borrower's bank account.
- **Borrower repays the loan:** The loan is usually due on the borrower's next payday. The borrower can repay the loan in full or make a minimum payment, usually including the interest and fees. If the borrower cannot repay the loan in full after their next paycheck, they may be able to roll over the loan by paying additional fees.

It's important to note that payday loans can have high-interest rates and fees, making them a costly option for borrowing money. Borrowers should only consider taking out a payday loan if they have exhausted all other options and can afford to repay the loan in full on their next payday.

Fees from $10 to $30 for every $100 borrowed are typical, and it's not uncommon for payday loan interest rates to exceed 20%. In addition, borrowers often get stuck in a cycle of taking out more loans to pay off the original loan, digging deeper into wealth-destroying debt.

Medical debt: According to Lending Tree, nearly half of all Americans have (or have had) medical debt. Worse, nearly one in four still do.[3] Medical expenses add up fast and are also one of the leading causes of bankruptcies. If you spend the night in a hospital room, your costs will skyrocket even more.

Gambling debt: Gambling debt is almost always bad debt, as it is often accompanied, just like credit cards and payday loans, by high-interest rates and fees. Gambling addiction can lead to a wicked cycle of debt, where the borrower takes out more loans to finance their habit.

Unpaid bills: Unpaid bills, such as utility or medical bills, can quickly become bad debt if not paid on time. Late fees and interest charges can accumulate, making it difficult to catch up on payments.

How to Get Out of Debt

If you have bad debt, then eliminating that debt should be your primary focus. So, let's spend the rest of this chapter discussing how to get out of debt and stay out of debt.

That's right, being debt free is a lifestyle. The habits you build and your decisions, without thinking about them, collectively make up your lifestyle. In this case, we're talk-

> *Getting out of debt is more than just a set of actions. It's a lifestyle.*

ing about habits that build wealth and decisions that prevent taking on bad debt. We will talk much more about these habits and decisions, but for now, just realize that your relationship with debt is a little more complicated than most people think.

But don't worry, getting out of it isn't. It just takes some time.

I've used the dieting analogy before, but let's use it again because it's that important. One-month diets don't produce long-lasting results. You might lose a few pounds during that month, but if you don't make that diet a part of your daily eating routine, you will likely pack those pounds right back onto your frame. You're back to where you started.

Ever watched the show *The Biggest Loser*? It was a TV reality show that pitted overweight contestants against each other to see which person could lose the most weight. Great in theory, but unfortunately, many contestants didn't make weight loss a part of their lifestyle and gained all that weight right back. In fact, a National Institutes of Health study followed 14 "Biggest Loser" contestants over six years and found that they gained all that weight back, and some even put on *more weight*.[4]

There is nothing different about getting out of debt. Yes, eliminating your bad debts is a wonderful thing. It's absolutely something you need to do ASAP. But if you don't change your lifestyle to stay out of debt, you're sentencing yourself (and your family) to a lifetime of digging yourselves out of financial holes. This isn't healthy!

So, let's talk about both of these concepts, starting with getting out of debt and then staying out of debt. Ready? Let's go.

If you have bad debts, your priority is to eliminate them. To do that, there are two key methods to murder those bad debts: Avalanche and Snowball. Both methods will eliminate your debt over time but attack debt repayment from very different perspectives.

The Debt Avalanche method prioritizes debts based on the interest rate. The Debt Snowball method prioritizes debts based on size.

Let's talk about each.

The Debt Avalanche Method

The Debt Avalanche method is a debt repayment strategy that focuses on paying off debts with the highest interest rates first while maintaining minimum payments on all other debts. The idea is to pay off high-interest debts first because those debts are costing you the most money (e.g. 20% interest rate costs you more money than a 4% interest rate).

Also known as "debt stacking," the primary goal of the Debt Avalanche method is to reduce the amount of interest paid over the life of the debts, which means you will pay off your debts faster and more efficiently than just randomly picking and choosing debts to repay.

Here's how the Debt Avalanche method works:

Step 1: List all your debts, including the total amount owed, the interest rate, and the minimum monthly payment.
Step 2: Sort all the debts by interest rate with the highest interest rate first.
Step 3: Make the minimum payments on all debts. Make additional payments on the first debt on your list (meaning, pay more than the minimum due, to slowly but surely eliminate the debt).
Step 4: Once each debt is paid off, take the same amount of money you paid for that debt and apply that as an additional payment to the next highest debt. Continue this process until all debts have been paid in full.

Consider this example of three debts ordered by interest rate:

Debt	Amount owned	Interest rate	Minimum payment
Visa card	$6,700	20%	$55
Car loan	$14,500	5.5%	$50
Student loan	$35,429	3.78%	$60

Notice that although the student loan is by far the biggest debt, the credit card debt is considered a top priority because it has the highest interest rate. Make minimum payments for all debts. Then, make additional payments to begin chipping away at your credit card debt until it's gone. Then focus on your car loan and then your student loans.

The Debt Avalanche method is considered an effective debt repayment strategy because it helps you save the most money in interest payments over the life of the debts. By prioritizing high-interest debts first, you can reduce the overall amount of interest paid over the life of the debts, which can lead to faster debt repayment.

As with everything in life, people should be aware of some potential drawbacks to the Debt Avalanche method before deciding to use this strategy.

For example, paying off debts with high-interest rates can take longer, which may demotivate some people. Additionally, if a person has a large debt with an equally large interest rate, they may be required to make large monthly payments that could strain their budget.

Despite these potential drawbacks, the Debt Avalanche method can be an effective debt repayment strategy for people with multiple high-interest debts who want to save money on interest payments. It can take discipline and focus to stick with this method, but the rewards can be significant.

Debt Avalanche Pros and Cons	
Pros:	Cons:
- Reduces total interest paid across all debts	- Requires more discipline
- Faster debt repayment	- Takes longer to see progress
- Forces discipline due to prioritizing high-interest debts first	- Could take more effort to order debts by interest rate (interest rates are not as obvious)

The Debt Snowball Method

The preferred method of well-known radio talk show host Dave Ramsey, the Debt Snowball method is a popular debt repayment strategy that involves prioritizing and paying off debts in order of size, beginning with the smallest debt.

The idea behind the Debt Snowball is to start with the smallest debt first and work toward the larger ones, building momentum as you pay off each debt. In this way, the Debt Snowball method aims to help people eliminate their debts more quickly by keeping their motivation high as debts are eliminated.

Step 1: List all your debts, including the total amount owed, the interest rate, and the minimum monthly payment.

Step 2: Sort all the debts by total remaining debt balance, smallest to biggest.

Step 3: Make the minimum payments on all debts. Make additional payments on the first debt on your list. Since this is your smallest debt, it likely won't take long to clear it off your list, giving you a mental win and motivation to move on to the next debt.

Step 4: Once each debt is paid off, take the same amount of money you paid for that debt and apply that as an additional payment to the next highest debt. Continue this process until all debts have been paid in full.

For example, if you have five debts with balances of $500, $1,000, $3,000, $7,000, and $10,000, you would first begin by focusing on paying off the $500 debt.

To start the Debt Snowball, you must pay the minimum monthly payment on all your debts except for the smallest balance, where you will pay as much as you can each month until that debt is paid off completely. This means you need to find extra money in your budget for that debt (hint: this should be one of the financial goals we discussed earlier). You can do this by cutting back on unnecessary expenses, finding ways to increase your income, or both.

Once you have paid off the smallest debt, you move on to the next smallest on your list. However, this time you will have more money to put towards it because you no longer have to make the minimum monthly payment on the debt you just paid off. Add that amount to the minimum payment for the next smallest debt on your list. This enables rapid debt repayment.

For example, if the minimum payment on the first debt was $50 but you paid $100 per month, you can now apply that $100 on top of the minimum payment on the next smallest debt. This allows you to pay off the second debt faster than the first.

As you continue to work through your list of debts, you will build momentum and motivation as you see each debt paid off. The Debt Snowball method helps to keep you focused on your goal of becoming debt free and gives you a sense of accomplishment with each debt you pay off.

The main advantage of the Debt Snowball method is motivation. Getting smaller wins under your belt by focusing on your smaller debts first may energize you and encourage you to keep going.

The method you choose is less important than just choosing one. Paying off your debts will help you build wealth and improve your credit score, which is used to qualify you for other loans (like an auto loan or a mortgage), insurance premiums, and even renting apartments. Some employers check credit scores as a routine part of their background checks before making job offers.

In other words, there is no downside to paying off your bad debts as soon as you can.

Debt Snowball Pros and Cons	
Pros:	Cons:
- Smaller wins may help keep you motivated to pay off debt	- Could take longer to pay off debt
- Simple to implement because you aren't worried about interest rates	- More total interest paid across all debts

How to Stay Out of Debt

As you learned before, staying out of debt is just as important as getting out of debt. Staying out of debt is a lifestyle choice, and it's not always easy. But the benefits of staying out of bad debt far outweigh the sacrifices it takes to get there.

First, let's be clear: I'm talking about staying out of *bad* debt, such as credit cards and gambling debts. Good debts—that is, borrowing money to improve yourself or to buy appreciating assets such as businesses and homes—still need to be carefully managed, but good debts aren't what I'm talking about in this section.

Staying out of bad debt requires a fundamental lifestyle change. It means we think about money differently and only use credit cards, for example, as a convenience rather than spending money we don't have (hint: there are many benefits to using credit cards responsibly). We understand that money is a tool; all tools are made to build something out of nothing.

For you, it might be buying that lake house you always wanted. Or moving to the Caribbean. Or maybe even early retirement.

The key to staying out of debt requires four fundamental things:

Identifying financial goals: As I discussed elsewhere in this book, having a reason to save and invest makes it more likely that you'll do it. For instance, saving a portion of your paycheck for that boat you want is probably easier than just "the future." The boat is a tangible goal. The future, on the other hand, isn't specific enough. Make your financial goals clear, specific, and achievable.

Paying yourself first: You learned in Habit #4 that the Pay Yourself First principle is a great way to meet your savings and investment goals, pay your bills, and enjoy a little zero-guilt spending. Paying yourself first makes it tougher to go into debt because you have put enough money aside to fund unexpected expenses, and you know exactly how much money you have left to spend on anything you want.

Tracking your spending: Keeping track of your spending is the only way to know if you're on the right track or if you're spending too much. There's literally no other way. Most millionaires at least have a general idea of how much they spend and where. If you notice that your spending is getting out of control, the spreadsheets you built back in Habit #9 will make it obvious and easy to fix.

Having an emergency fund: Without an e-fund, you risk debt if you are caught with an unexpected expense such as a car accident, medical bill, or even job loss. Keeping a little money set aside in a savings account provides a buffer in case you need extra cash whenever life happens.

Take Action: Here's What You Need to Do

Step 1: Identify your bad debts. Again, your bad debts include things such as credit cards, payday loans, and other debts for things that are *not* appreciating assets. Hint: These debts also tend to have high-interest rates, which you want to prioritize paying off as quickly as possible.

Step 2: Decide on a pay-off plan. Whether you choose the Debt Avalanche or Snowball Method (or another type of debt repayment plan), make it your #1 priority to eliminate your bad debts, as those debts are murdering your chances of building wealth and becoming a millionaire.

Step 3: Then continue tracking. Tracking is crucial. If you don't track your money, you are 10x more likely to go into debt.

Notes

1. "Money Causes the Most Stress for Couples, According to New Ally Survey." Ally Financial (2018). https://www.prnewswire.com/news-releases/money-causes-the-most-stress-for-couples-according-to-new-ally-survey-300664794.html.

2. Olya, G. "Jaw-Dropping Stats About the State of Debt in America." Yahoo Finance (2023). https://finance.yahoo.com/news/jaw-dropping-stats-state-credit-130022967.html.

3. Delfino, D. "23% of Americans Have Medical Debt (and Other Stats)." Lending Tree (2022). https://www.lendingtree.com/personal/medical-debt-statistics.

4. Fothergill, Erin, Juen Guo, Lilian Howard, Jennifer C. Kerns, Nicolas D. Knuth, Robert Brychta, Kong Y. Chen et al. "Persistent Metabolic Adaptation 6 Years after 'The Biggest Loser' Competition." *Obesity* 24, no. 8 (2016): 1612–1619. https://pubmed.ncbi.nlm.nih.gov/27136388/.

Part 2

How to FIRE
What Is Financial Independence Retire Early?

I n Part 1 of this book, you learned about the 10 habits of millionaires. These habits will help get you rich over time. But why? Why do you want to get rich? Just because?

Probably not.

Imagine having all the money in the world but not knowing what to do. If you're like most people (me included!), without a reason for building wealth, you will start spending that money on the wrong things just because you have it.

The idea behind building wealth is the freedom to do what you truly want to do, even if that means spending more time outside of an office. Freedom over your time is the ultimate freedom, and the

FIRE movement has taken this concept by storm to achieve some truly miraculous things. It's caught mass media attention.

In fact, my wife and I have been featured in video segments from CBS *MarketWatch* and CNBC and countless articles across the Internet.

In Part 2, we will discuss FIRE in detail. You will learn what it is, whether it's right for you, and—if it is right for you—how to achieve it using the millionaire habits from Part 1.

Trust me, this is the fun part. This is where we get to enjoy the fruits of our labor.

First, let me tell you a story. It begins on a sunbaked Saturday morning in spring 13 years ago. I lived in a suburban house south of Tucson, Arizona. As a single highly paid software developer, I had all the creature comforts of life. You know, the things that portray wealth and success. I went to work every day, did my job, and then came home, eager to forget about the mountain of work I had in front of me the next day.

That Saturday morning, I walked into my garage and robotically reached up to punch the door opener. I've done this thousands of times before without even thinking about it. But on this Saturday, something was different.

For some reason, I froze. My hand never got to the garage door opener. Instead, I turned around and looked at what was sitting there in front of me.

On the left was my brand new Cadillac CTS. In the middle sat my Yamaha R1 sport bike, a motorcycle that cost me $220/month for insurance as a 28-year-old kid. And on the right was my arctic white supercharged Corvette convertible. I had it all, complete with expensive and life-threatening adrenaline-packed toys in my garage, ready to help me forget about a life that wasn't making me happy.

Instead of opening the garage door, I stood there and looked at the money I was spending on everything. Sure, I had fun driving those cars and riding the motorcycle, but those things did nothing to overcome a career draining my life.

How could someone with all this stuff still feel unfulfilled? I felt something was missing, but I couldn't put the pieces together.

That Saturday morning was the first time I admitted to myself that my choices were wrong. Very wrong. At the time, I didn't have everything figured out. In fact, far from it. But that weekend was a turning point in my outlook on money and life. I needed a way out. I was determined to find a way to quit my job and spend the rest of my life doing something that truly made me happy.

I didn't know it then, but FIRE was the solution.

Financial Independence Retire Early—or FIRE—is a two-part concept.

First, **financial independence**. The "FI" part of the acronym means you've saved and invested enough money never to have to earn another dollar again for the rest of your life. Through the power of compound interest and keeping your expenses low, FI means you can live solely off the capital gains of your investments.

Your money is *really* working for you.

Note that just because you're financially independent doesn't mean you have to quit your job. If you enjoy working, there's nothing wrong with doing just that. FI means you don't have to work but may choose to anyway. In other words, it gives you options.

Second, **retire early**. After achieving financial independence, the next step of quitting your job and retiring early completes the "FIRE" acronym. This means you've decided to quit working and live off your investment income for the rest of your life.

At this point, you might have a couple of questions for me: *"How much do I need to have invested?"* or *"What if the market goes down and my capital gains drop?"*

Don't worry, we'll get to those questions. There are a lot of misconceptions about what it means to FIRE and how it's done, and we'll clear it all up in the next couple of chapters.

Within the FIRE community, my story isn't all that unique. But among the larger population, it's extremely unique (and, to some people, pretty crazy).

From the moment I set foot in an office, I knew this wasn't for me. I couldn't stand the performance reviews, the useless meetings, the meaningless mission statements, the coworkers who thought they were experts at everything. . .

But for more than 14 years, I endured it anyway. I rose through the ranks. I switched companies and got raises. I learned valuable skills. Even still, I knew being in corporate America until age 65 wasn't my place.

At such a young age, I had no concept of financial independence or early retirement. Like most people, I didn't know exactly what I wanted. But I knew exactly what I *didn't want*, and that was a 40-year career working in drab office buildings and working on other people's problems.

Things started to get real when I met the woman who would eventually become my wife. She's a rocket scientist (yes, literally) and made similar money as me. We pulled in a little over $200,000 by the end of our careers. This was in 2013, when pulling down 200 Gs was a lot of money. Life-changing money.

We had a decision to make. With a relatively high salary, we could either:

Live like rockstars. This was the fun route. I'm talking about big vacation homes, driving around in expensive luxury cars, expensive dinners, season tickets, you name it. We could enjoy the nicer things in life and spend money like it was going out of style.

Save, invest, and quit work. The alternative to living like a rockstar is saving and investing most of what we earn to build wealth rapidly. With that wealth, we could quit our jobs and pursue a lifestyle that, you know, interested us!

I'm sure you know which one we chose.

For years, my wife and I saved 70 percent of our combined salaries (and if you're doing the math, 70 percent of over $200,000 is a ton of money).

Here's exactly what we did:

- Maxed our employee-sponsored 401(k), which was $17,000 at the time;
- Maxed our Roth IRAs, which was $5,500 at the time;
- Then, we opened a Vanguard brokerage account and funneled over $100,000 a year into index funds to exploit the power of the

stock market even more. We made this easy by using monthly automated routines to invest every month.

- We tracked our spending meticulously. We got to the point where my wife could tell you how much we spent on sweet potatoes for years! While you don't need to go to quite this level of detail, we did.

We barreled toward financial independence as fast as we possibly could.

For three years, we lived like college students and socked away hundreds of thousands of dollars, rapidly accumulating enough wealth until we finally said, "Let's do this."

And so we did. We quit our jobs, sold our house, and traveled the United States full-time in an Airstream RV. We learned a lot about our country by traveling, and the memories we made are something that I wouldn't trade for anything.

I'm not saying you must sell your house and live in a trailer to achieve financial independence and retire early. This is just our story.

But I won't tell you that achieving financial independence is easy, either. It's not.

Financial independence requires a purposeful and conscious lifestyle. Your spending can't be out of control. Avoid credit card debt at all costs. Without discipline, achieving financial independence, especially early on, will be extremely difficult—if not impossible. It needs to be more important than spending money on other things.

Financial independence requires many years of earning a progressively higher income, saving and investing that income, and controlling spending. Very few people achieve financial freedom overnight unless they win the lottery or get a huge windfall. Instead, it requires years of dedication and focus. It's simple, but it doesn't happen quickly.

If you harbor dreams of financial independence early in life, increasing your income should be your priority (unless you have high-interest debts such as credit cards, in which case getting rid of that debt should be your top priority). Ways to boost your income and pay off bad debt are discussed at length in Part 1.

Okay, that's out of the way. In the next chapter, we'll talk about exactly how this works, including answers to those two questions that you probably asked earlier in this chapter.

The Simple Math
Behind FIRE

I'll start this chapter with an admission of guilt: math was never my strong suit. If I got a B in my algebra classes in school, I would be the happiest kid in the class.

But luckily, you don't need to be a math major to add up how FIRE works.

And that's exactly what we're going to do in this chapter. Understanding how much money you need before reaching financial freedom is a critical data point because it gives you a clear and defined target to shoot for.

We need to understand the math (don't worry, it's easy).

But before we do, we must discuss an important element of this equation: net worth.

Your net worth is a straightforward calculation of assets minus your liabilities. This number is considered to be what you are "worth" financially.

To find your net worth, add all your assets, including your savings, investments, cash, real estate, vehicles, and the equity in your home. Then, add up all of your liabilities, including your remaining mortgage, debts, credit card spending, and other loans or financial obligations. Then, do the math:

$$\text{Assets} - \text{liabilities} = \text{net worth}$$

Note that your net worth can be negative if you have more liabilities than assets. For instance, if you have \$75,000 of assets but \$100,000 in liabilities, your net worth is –\$25,000. Obviously, that's not where we want to be. We want our net worth to be positive (and as far in the positive territory as we can get it!).

You don't necessarily need to know your net worth today. However, you will need to find that number before reaching the point of financial freedom.

Note that some don't include their primary residence as part of their net worth, arguing you still need to live somewhere. In other words, cash from selling your primary residence will most likely be spent on another primary residence. Because you cannot keep the home sale proceeds, some argue, it shouldn't be included in your net worth.

However, this is wrong. Remember that the equity in your home is an asset. While it's true that home sale proceeds will probably be spent on another primary residence, the equity you have in your home is a non-liquid asset.

When Have You Achieved FIRE?

You've achieved FIRE (or just "You've FIRE'd," for short) when your investments return enough capital gains to pay all of your living expenses. In other words, you can live off your investment returns without earning employment income.

For instance, if you spend \$80,000 a year, your capital gains and other investment returns must fully fund your \$80,000 lifestyle. In this case, your investments need to provide at least \$80,000 a year in gains.

Now let's get into some math. There are two ways that most FIRE'ees calculate when they have achieved financial independence. Thanks to the Trinity study, the math is actually quite simple. What's the Trinity study?

Conducted by three professors from Trinity University in 1998, the Trinity study is a well-known retirement simulation that studied the sustainability of withdrawal rates from a retirement portfolio over a 30-year time horizon.[1]

In other words, the purpose of the study was to reveal a safe withdrawal rate so retirees can maintain their existing standard of living without running out of money.

The study looked at different withdrawal rates, ranging from 3 to 12 percent and examined their success rates over different rolling 30-year periods of historical stock market returns. The study included the 1929 Great Depression.

The Trinity researchers found that a 4% withdrawal rate was generally sustainable over a 30-year retirement period, assuming a balanced portfolio of stocks and bonds.

This means that retirees could withdraw 4% of their initial retirement portfolio balance when they retire and adjust the amount annually for inflation while standing a good chance of never running out of money during their retirement years.

The Trinity study has become a widely cited benchmark for retirement planning and has helped shape how financial planners and retirees think about retirement income planning.

There are two primary ways to do the math using the Trinity study's 4% guideline:

Method #1: Multiply your current net worth by 0.04. This reveals how much money you can spend every year in retirement.
Method #2: Multiply your yearly spending by 25. This reveals how much money you need before achieving financial independence.

Both of these methods give you the same answer but from different angles. The method you choose depends on what number you want to base the calculation on, your existing net worth, or the amount of money you spend annually.

For instance, let's assume you have a $500,000 net worth. Using method #1, you can only spend $20,000 a year in retirement. We got this math by running this calculation:

$$500000 \times 0.04$$

For those living in the industrialized world, spending just $20,000 a year isn't possible. In this situation, we're not yet financially independent.

However, let's stay we have $1,000,000. Now we can spend $40,000 a year. While still low, some low-cost-of-living areas of the country (and the world) may allow for that type of low-cost lifestyle, making us financially independent *in those areas of the world*.

In other words, you might be financially independent in a small Kansas town, but you won't be financially independent in New York City. Your cost of living (aka your location and lifestyle choices) is an important element of this equation.

Let's run another calculation. This time, we will start with how much we spend yearly to determine how much we need before becoming financially independent.

Assume we spend $78,000 a year. This includes all expenses, including our mortgage or rent, utilities, clothes, cell phones, and so forth.

The math looks like this:

$$78,000 \times 25 = 1,950,000.$$

Using the Trinity study's 4% rule, we need almost $2 million to maintain our $78,000 annual spending and be financially independent.

This tells us a couple of things about achieving financial independence:

First, financial independence is governed by your net worth and cost of living.

This means in a scenario where two people have the same net worth, one might be financially independent while the other isn't because of the cost of living where they live.

Second, just because you're financially independent doesn't mean you've FIRE'd.

Remember, there's the "RE" part, too. FIRE assumes that you "retire early" after achieving financial independence rather than continue working a job. If you quit your job and live the rest of your life off your investment returns, congratulations, you've just FIRE'd!

"Steve, if I'm financially independent, why would I NOT retire?"

That is a good question, and there's an equally good answer. Early retirement is not for everyone. In fact, it can be a devastating choice for some people. In the next chapter, I'll discuss why early retirement may not be the right answer. For now, let's assume that early retirement is right for you. You're looking to escape the workforce fast.

I am a fan of using the Trinity study to do the back-of-the-napkin calculations for early retirement, but keep in mind the study's inherent limitations.

The Trinity study's limitations include:

Historical data bias: We've all heard the phrase "past performance does not guarantee future results," and it's true with the Trinity study. Economic conditions and market trends change significantly, affecting the sustainability of withdrawal rates.

Limited time horizon: People live longer today than they did 30 years ago (men live about 75 years, on average, and women live to be about 80). The study only examined withdrawal rates over a 30-year retirement period, which may not be sufficient for those planning longer retirements.

Simplistic assumptions: The study assumed a fixed withdrawal rate and an asset allocation of half-and-half stocks to bonds. Retirees may need to adjust their withdrawal rate, asset allocation, and risk tolerance based on personal circumstances, market conditions, and other factors.

Ignoring taxes and fees: The study did not account for taxes, expense ratios, transaction costs, and management fees, which can significantly affect the sustainability of withdrawal rates (and reinforce why passive investments, which often require lower fees, are generally superior to actively managed funds).

Non-uniformity in the sample: The study used only one type of retiree, a US household with fixed annual consumption. This may not apply to different types of households in different regions.

Even with these limitations, the 4% rule is a solid starting point for figuring out how much money you need to accumulate before quitting your job and sipping cocktails on the beach for a living.

You Can Fall Out of Financial Independence

Let me assume the role of the buzzkill for a moment. Your job isn't done after achieving financial freedom. If your expenses increase (or investment returns decrease), you can fall out of financial independence.

Obviously, this is something we want to avoid at all costs. Luckily, there are techniques that can be used to ensure you don't spend yourself out of financial freedom.

First, redo the math at least once a year.

My wife and I redo the Trinity calculations every year to ensure we are still on track and staying true to our spending budget. We adjust our spending when necessary to ensure we aren't spending more than anticipated.

For instance, we might spend a little more money when the market is up and cut back when the market is down. After seven years of early retirement, we have a pretty good idea of how much we can spend from year to year, and you will too.

Second, make sure your spending isn't higher than you think.

After reaching financial freedom, you must stay focused and reconfirm your "*freedom status*" periodically. As we discussed in Habit #9, keeping a spending budget will help reveal any spending overages or unanticipated expenses from month to month. If you spend more in a certain category than you thought, that's okay. Address why and make the appropriate adjustments.

Third, keep the lines of communication open.

Talking about money with your spouse is critical. Though it's not always easy, an open line of communication will help you and your spouse stay on the same page regarding financial goals, spending choices, and overall happiness.

Refer to my bonus chapter, "How to Talk to Your Spouse about Money" for ideas on keeping the lines of communication between you and your spouse open.

Note

1. "Trinity Study." Wikipedia. `https://en.wikipedia.org/wiki/Trinity_study`.

Health Care in Retirement

If you decide that retiring early is right for you, one of the biggest questions you'll likely have is health care. That is: *"Is there an affordable health care option?"*

Traditionally, health care has been a big reason why more millionaires don't retire early, and this is especially true with kids—because health care is more complicated and expensive if you have children. Unfortunately, affordable and high-quality health care in the United States is tied to employment. And because most early retirees aren't old enough to qualify for Medicare, health insurance options sometimes seem limited.

But because you're reading this book, you are privy to the real truth behind health care in retirement: it's not only possible but also easy.

The Affordable Care Act's health care marketplace makes it easy for early retirees to get health care that isn't ridiculously expensive, depending on your health requirements. But the Affordable Care Act isn't the only way early retirees find health coverage.

In this chapter, we'll discuss your retirement health care options, including a health coverage option that isn't technically health insurance.

In fact, let's start with that one.

Healthshares

Healthshare programs aren't health insurance, but they operate in a similar fashion. Also known as "healthshare ministries" or "cost-sharing" programs, healthshares are an alternative to traditional health insurance where members of the healthshare share the cost of medical expenses.

In a healthshare, each member pays monthly dues, similar to a premium with traditional health care. These dues are used to cover the medical expenses of the members who have eligible health care needs, minus the "unshared amount," which is the amount that members must pay before the healthshare will reimburse. This is similar to your deductible with health insurance.

After a member receives medical treatment or services, they submit their medical bills to the healthshare organization for reimbursement.

Once a medical bill is submitted, the healthshare verifies eligibility of the expenses and reimburses the member for all qualified expenses. The reimbursement money comes from the collective pot that all members contribute monthly.

Some hospitals work directly with the healthshare provider, but others don't. Those members are considered cash-paying patients if a hospital doesn't work directly with a healthshare. Believe it or not, some hospitals offer discounts to cash-paying patients.

It's important to note that healthshares are not insurance companies and are not regulated similarly. They are often based on faith-based principles and may require members to adhere to certain religious beliefs or lifestyle choices. Additionally, unlike traditional health insurance, healthshares do not guarantee payment or have the same legal obligations for coverage. For instance, healthshares can deny those with preexisting conditions and refuse to cover costs associated with bad habits or recklessness, such as smoking or skydiving accidents.

Each healthshare organization may have its own guidelines, eligibility criteria, and limitations on coverage. Therefore, it's crucial for individuals considering healthshares to thoroughly research and understand the specific terms and conditions before joining.

The benefit of healthshares is they can be substantially less expensive than traditional health care. However, they can do whatever they want since they aren't governed by the same laws as health insurance companies. This means healthshares are often cheaper, but that does come with a few major downsides.

Here are the pros and cons of healthshares:

Pros	Cons
Price: Healthshares are usually cheaper than traditional health insurance, making it easier for early retirees to find affordable health coverage.	**It's not insurance:** Healthshares are not the same as insurance and aren't governed by the same rules and regulations of traditional health care.
No out-of-network restrictions: Healthshares let members see any provider without out-of-network restrictions common with health insurance.	**Preexisting conditions:** Healthshares are not obligated to cover members with existing conditions or certain medical treatments not in line with the faith-based values of the organization.
Faith-based: For members of faith, sharing costs among like-minded people can bring a sense of shared values.	**Requires work:** Members are required to submit their bills to the healthshare if the hospital doesn't work with the share.
	Out-of-pocket costs: If the hospital doesn't work directly with your healthshare, you will need to cover the hospital bill, submit payment receipts to the healthshare, and hope you get reimbursed in a timely fashion.

Full disclosure, my wife and I started with a healthshare program but switched to traditional health insurance after the Affordable Care Act established the health care marketplace. This drastically reduced health care costs due to subsidies (more below). These subsidies make it easier for early retirees to find affordable health care.

Traditional Health Care

The Affordable Care Act's (ACA) health care marketplace has made traditional health insurance much more affordable for retirees. This is because subsidies (also known as premium tax credits) are refundable tax credits available for those with a low income, which most early retirees are, even though they have a high net worth. This can save you hundreds of dollars monthly with reduced-cost health insurance premiums.

To be eligible for the premium tax credit, you must meet certain requirements:

- Must be a US citizen or lawful permanent resident;
- Must have an income below 400% of the federal poverty level;
- Must not be eligible for employer-sponsored health insurance;
- Must not be eligible for Medicare or Medicaid.

Your net worth is not a factor in eligibility. This means that early retirees with $2 million in net worth may still qualify for low-income subsidies due to not earning a salary.

Exact subsidized coverage limits change constantly, so refer to healthcare.gov for the latest requirements and limitations for subsidies and premium tax credits.

If you have a preexisting condition, you will probably find choosing a health plan from the ACA's health care marketplace easier than a healthshare, which isn't governed by the same rules and regulations as traditional health insurance companies. In other words, healthshare programs are not required to cover preexisting conditions. To keep costs down, many don't.

You can sign up for an ACA health plan during the annual open enrollment period at healthcare.gov. Note that some states have their own marketplace website.

COBRA

COBRA, or Consolidated Omnibus Budget Reconciliation Act, is a way to temporarily stay on your employer's health insurance plan after you retire. Typically, COBRA lets you remain on your health plan for 18 months, though it can be extended after a major life event such as another job loss, marriage or divorce, or death.

To be eligible for COBRA, you must have been covered by your employer's health insurance plan for at least 50 full calendar weeks (not consecutive) during the previous 12 months.

You must also have lost your coverage through one of the qualifying events:

- Voluntary or involuntary job loss;
- Reduction in hours;
- Spouse's job loss;
- Death of a covered employee;
- Divorce or legal separation;
- Marriage;
- Birth or adoption of a child;
- Loss of eligibility for Medicare or Medicaid.

Sound like a good deal? Well, there's a catch. Using COBRA to remain on your employer's health plan will cost you a lot more money than before.

Since your employer will no longer subsidize the plan, you'll be responsible for the entire monthly premium (plus a 2% administrative fee), making COBRA more of an option for short-term health coverage. For instance, COBRA can help bridge the gap between your old and new jobs, but it won't be a good long-term health insurance option.

Medicaid

Another option is Medicaid, a US government–subsidized option for those with incomes below 138 percent of the federal poverty level in most states.

Whether you qualify for health coverage through Medicaid depends on your state and whether your state expanded coverage after the enactment of the Affordable Care Act. Some states only look at your household income for access to Medicaid, while others also consider disabilities and family size.

Medicaid coverage is typically less common among younger retirees but can be an option for some people who qualify in their state.

No Health Insurance

As of January 2019, there is no federal mandate for health insurance in the United States. However, a few states require health coverage, such as California, New Jersey, Massachusetts, Rhode Island, and Vermont. That means you don't have to buy health insurance if you live outside those states.

While it might seem like a way to save money, it's also extremely risky. Without some type of health coverage, you're paying for all medical expenses yourself. Overnight stays in a hospital can easily reach $10,000 or more a night, depending on the level of care you need. If you need to be airlifted to a hospital after a car accident, that's another couple thousand if it's a short flight. One couple paid nearly $500,000 for an air transport flight from Colorado to North Carolina![1]

Without health coverage, you'll be on the hook to pay for all that in cash.

Even if you're in good health, I always recommend health coverage for everyone, whether that's a healthshare, a plan on the ACA, or Medicaid. Ensure you're covered for life's unexpected medical costs, which are *never* cheap and can cause a tremendous amount of debt if you need expensive health care without being covered. Remember, Habit #10 discussed the importance of staying out of debt and how tough it can be to become a millionaire if you're digging yourself out of debt.

Note

1. Berlin, S. "Bill for Hospital Helicopter Ride Sparks Anger." *Newsweek* (2022). https://www.newsweek.com/bill-hospital-helicopter-ride-sparks-anger-1730580.

The Different
Flavors of FIRE

The term "FIRE" is a very high-level phrase that describes an insanely wide range of lifestyle choices on the way to (and after) reaching financial independence. As I said in the introduction of this book, you don't have to sell your house and set sail in an RV to FIRE, as my wife and I did. We wanted to adventure around the country, but it won't be for everyone.

There are a lot of unique ways to live your early retirement lifestyle.

And because people love acronyms, there's generally an abbreviation for every one of these lifestyles. Don't laugh, because some of them are quite funny.

Let's take a look at the most common types of FIRE lifestyles:

TraditionalFIRE

As the name suggests, this type of FIRE is common with most early retirees. This type of lifestyle generally is for people who spend between **$41,000 and $99,000** a year.

Traditional FIRE'ees invest most of their money in the stock market, real estate, and other investment classes. They live comfortably but not extravagantly. They might plan the occasional pricey vacation or cruise but probably aren't jet-setting worldwide yearly (unless they use credit card or house-hacking techniques that can drastically reduce the cost of international travel).

The cost of living for traditional FIRE'ees is average. In fact, your lifestyle might not look much different than it did when you were working (minus the work part, of course). No major changes in spending. A lot of early retirees are in this category.

This type of FIRE, along with the following two, also assumes decades of working high-paying jobs and getting consistent raises and promotions, aggressive savings and investment, and pushing off higher-priced purchases until much later in life.

LeanFIRE

LeanFIRE is for those who want to retire as soon as possible and don't care about spending much money after retirement. LeanFIRE folks often spend less than **$40,000** a year, which is still possible in many areas of the United States. However, this probably means living outside a major metropolitan area where the cost of living is high.

LeanFIRE folks heavily control their spending. They don't go out to eat much, take pricey vacations, upgrade their cell phones every year, or buy new cars very often. They also tend to work demanding but high-paying jobs to rapidly accumulate enough wealth to quit their jobs and retire as early in life as possible.

You probably wouldn't know these folks are early retired at all, other than the fact they seem to be enjoying their lives more than the typical person by shopping at 10 a.m. on a Tuesday, jogging in the park in the middle of the day, and having no real concept of what day of the week it is.

FatFIRE

If you want to spend more than **$100,000** a year in early retirement, you're in the FatFIRE category. This type of FIRE allows for an upper-middle class lifestyle that includes substantially more spending than LeanFIRE.

According to the Trinity math discussed in Chapter 11, FatFIRE will require about $2,500,000 in net worth to spend $100K a year. Generally, FatFIRE folks work higher-paying jobs or are willing to work longer to achieve a higher-end lifestyle. Or both! FatFIRE is common with doctors, software engineers, lawyers, and others who worked for many years in a high-income career field and don't want to reduce their lifestyle after retirement.

People in this category don't need to make as many sacrifices to their lifestyle after quitting their jobs, including traveling, restaurants, entertainment, and living in higher cost-of-living areas of the country.

CoastFIRE

CoastFIRE is a unique approach that lets you continue to work jobs you enjoy without the stress often associated with a high salary in a demanding job. In other words, this strategy is more about financial independence than early retirement. It balances financial independence with personal fulfillment. You won't reach financial freedom as quickly, but you won't need to endure decades of stressful work.

In CoastFIRE, you front-load your earnings early in your career by working a high-paying job and investing aggressively, often 50% or more of your income. Once you reach a certain net worth level, you can quit that demanding career for a less stressful job, live off of a lower salary, and let your investments "coast" to your targeted retirement number.

For instance, let's assume you need $1 million to reach financial independence. You will spend a handful of years working your butt off in a high-paying career field and getting raises and promotions to continuously increase your salary. You might sacrifice your social life during this phase to save on entertainment-related expenses like weekly bar runs, movies, new cars, and expensive vacations. You're saving and investing hard for these years, prioritizing your future lifestyle over your present one.

After 10 years, you've accumulated $600,000. Now, you pull your foot off the gas pedal and take a lower-stress job in a career field that interests you. Instead of working a $150,000-a-year job and investing every penny you can, you only make $70,000 and stop investing altogether. But your $600,000 nest egg continues to grow year after year in the market while you live off of your $70,000.

Now, you'll take more vacations. Spend more money socially. In other words, you live a more normal life in a career field you enjoy without having to worry as much about saving and investing for retirement because you already have a growing nest egg.

BaristaFIRE

BaristaFIRE is very similar to CoastFIRE, but with one major difference. You're not yet financially independent with the CoastFIRE strategy. Instead, you're front-loading your career earnings and then backing off for a more enjoyable life as your investments continue to grow in the market.

With BaristaFIRE, however, you're already financially independent but you continue to work part-time (as a barista at a coffee shop, for instance), mainly for the benefits, such as less expensive health insurance. Working part-time may bring in $20,000 to $30,000 a year in additional income, too. You don't *need* the income, but it's nice.

You might withdraw a small amount of money each month from your investments to help supplement your part-time income. This strategy assumes the benefits you get with a part-time job outweigh the drawback of potentially using some of your investments to fund your lifestyle because you're no longer working in your full-time career.

This type of FIRE is like dipping your toes into the early retirement pool without diving in head first. You're technically there from a net worth perspective, but you still work part-time for the benefits and to make your lifestyle just a bit nicer or easier.

HybridFIRE

The last type of FIRE is basically "whatever the hell you want." Many choose to pursue a combination of these FIRE types so it fits their lifestyle and risk tolerance.

For instance, maybe you'll work hard and save aggressively until you reach half of your net worth number for retirement. Then, you take a CoastFIRE approach by letting your investments continue to build in the market while you work a less stressful job to fully fund your lifestyle. Once you reach financial independence, you use the BaristaFIRE approach by working a low-stress part-time job for the benefits and additional income that you don't technically need, but it's still nice to have anyway.

The point here is there's no requirement to follow any of these strategies to the T. Find the type of FIRE that works best for you and your family, and be open to switching things up as changes happen.

What surprised me the most about early retirement is how many opportunities there are out there that you never knew existed when I worked a full-time job. My mind subconsciously ignored these options because I already worked a good job and didn't need the additional income (or stress).

But look at me now. I'm writing this book. I'm also a freelance personal finance writer for a few online publications. I also teach cohort-style online classes about how to grow and make money on social media.

I never thought I would be making money after quitting my full-time career, but rolling with the punches and saying yes to opportunities (remember Habit #1?) generates income even when you don't need it.

Debunking the Criticisms of FIRE

S trangely, those pursuing FIRE can get a lot of hate. I know I have! I've been called every name in the book, accused of living off the fat of the land and being lazy, unproductive, and a mooch on society. And those are the only criticisms tame enough to be allowed in this book!

People always criticize the idea of FIRE (and those pursuing it). It's human nature, isn't it? Humans tend to assume the worst whenever someone is blazing a path against the norm. Some of these criticisms are legitimate. But, I've found that many are rooted in jealousy. Most people want the freedom that comes from FIRE.

Not everyone will be able to achieve it.

In this chapter, I will debunk many of the criticisms of FIRE. But fair warning: I will be honest in each answer rather than just cherry-pick the positive side of FIRE and ignore the negative. This is going to be your dose of reality. If you dream of quitting your job early and pursuing a life of freedom and adventure outside of an office, do yourself a favor and read the rest of this chapter.

"You're not contributing to society if you're retired."

This is a fascinating criticism, and it assumes that we can only make a difference in our communities by working a job. The entire premise is as confusing as it is wrong.

In fact, I'd argue precisely the opposite.

Not working full-time gives us *more time* to give back and impact society. I know an early retiree who volunteers at a local animal shelter. Others volunteer at soup kitchens, help their friends move, tutor local children, and spend more time with their families. There are an unlimited number of ways we can give back to our communities and positively impact society when we no longer have that full-time job.

This argument is exactly backward. Early retirees have more time to contribute to society than most people working full-time. That doesn't mean all early retirees will choose to spend their time volunteering and bettering society, but they probably have the time and energy to do so if they want. And that's the whole point of early retirement.

We get to spend more time doing the things that are important to us.

"Don't you get bored?"

This criticism is rooted in some truth. As I discuss in the next chapter, boredom is a real possibility in early retirement unless you have something you're retiring to, not just from. For instance, most of us understand that we're retiring from a career we don't like (or a boss we can't stand!). That part is generally clear.

That's not the whole story. When each day is no longer filled with the demands of working a full-time job, it's your responsibility to fill each day. For some, it'll be easy. But for others, that thought might be terrifying. You can only binge-watch so much Netflix before you realize that you still need something to do with your life. You need a purpose.

For most of us, our jobs fill that role. After the job, you need to find purpose in your life another way. It might be volunteering in your community. Or maybe now's the time to write that book you've always wanted to write.

I recommend not quitting your job until you know what you will do with your time outside your full-time career. You don't need to have every detail worked out, but a general idea of what will fill your time and sense of purpose will help you ease into your new early retired lifestyle.

"You're not retired if you make money."

If you claim to be retired but dare to make money by doing something you love, be prepared for attacks from what I like to call the "*retirement police.*"

The *retirement police* is an often hostile group of people who accuse FIREees of not being retired if they still earn money, regardless of the amount. If you earn any money in retirement, this group will claim you're not actually retired.

I've gotten this many times. After I released my first eBook, the social media comments almost immediately started:

"So, not retired then. . ."
"If you're rich, why are you selling an eBook?"
"Sounds like you just switched careers rather than retired."

In the end, it doesn't matter what the retirement police think. The younger you retire, the more likely you'll do *something* in retirement that earns you money. You might be surprised at how many money-making opportunities there are after you quit your nine-to-five job. If you have a marketable skill, society wants you!

How you define retirement is ultimately up to you. But consider this: If a 70-year-old grandpa loves woodworking and occasionally sells wooden furniture, I doubt many would accuse Gramps of being a retirement fraud or working a career. If a 40-year-old does the same, suddenly, the retirement police throw the metaphorical cuffs out and accuse the poor soul of lying about his or her retirement.

"You'll never be able to get your job back if things go wrong."

You're right, I won't. But why would I want the same job back that I spent so many years trying to escape? The last thing I want is to go back to the career that drove me to early retirement in the first place.

The thrust behind this criticism is true: the longer you're out of the workforce, the less likely you'll be able to reenter it, making the same salary. Why? Because in most industries, things change. And that resume gap might put you at a disadvantage compared to other candidates with more recent experience in your field.

Here's why this doesn't matter. If things go poorly (unexpected expenses, medical bills, recession, etc.), you'll probably realize what's happening before you're forced back to work. You can make spending adjustments before things get bad, including selling your home and moving to a lower-cost-of-living area.

Moreover, you probably won't need to work a stressful, high-paying job again anyway to make ends meet. After all, you retired early by controlling your spending and taking full advantage of your nine-to-five job. You understand how to earn and save. And you won't be starting at zero, either. Instead, you might adopt the principles of CoastFIRE (discussed in the previous chapter) to let your investments continue to grow as you work a less stressful job to fund your day-to-day living expenses.

And so, you're right! I won't be able to get that same job back, but that's okay.

I don't want that job back.

"There is no way your money will last in *this* market!"

Early retirement is easy when stocks are up during a bull market. Nobody blinks an eye at the capital gains you reap when times are good. But when the market turns south, the FIRE haters suddenly reemerge from the woodwork, ready to pounce.

The biggest fear most early retirees have (and retirees in general) is running out of money. For most of us, that's the worst-case scenario. But according to the data, the opposite is happening. That is, most retirees *aren't spending enough*.

A recent Employee Benefit Research Institute study found that nearly 75 percent of retirees between the ages of 62 and 75 have seen their assets stay the same or grow in retirement.[1] Most retirees are being so conservative in their retirement that their portfolios tend to go up, rather than down, after calling it quits from full-time work.

This isn't to say that you should spend like a drunken sailor in retirement. I am telling you this to help you understand that the worst-case scenario happens quite rarely.

When I quit in 2016, people told me I would be back to work within five years. There's no way our nest egg of around a million will last. "A million is nothing!" they'd say.

Yet, seven years later, we're doing just fine. Even with the down market and recession fears of 2022 and 2023, our portfolio has grown since quitting our careers seven years ago.

We used the Trinity math to estimate how much money we needed to retire early, and it worked out. Through the market's ups and downs, our money always has a way of normalizing once again. We might spend a little more when the market is up and less when the market is down. The important part is we don't time the market. We never buy because we think stock prices have bottomed out, and we don't sell because prices are up. We've kept our money in the market since 2016, and despite bear markets and recession fears that permeate our economic climate in 2023, the market has boosted our net worth by more than $200,000 since saying goodbye to our careers.

But let's be real: It is possible that your money won't last. Maybe the market takes a drastic dip, or you get into a car accident requiring years of expensive medical care. Things happen, and we can't always control these things. The one thing we can control is having an emergency fund for unexpected expenses, tracking our spending so we don't go overboard, and keeping in touch with our personal and professional network so we have a few good friends to lean on if we need a favor.

"You're wasting everything you've worked for!"

This criticism will be deeply personal. It will depend on your situation and your educational background. For instance, a medical doctor who retires 10 years after medical school might seem like a waste of schooling (not to mention the debt that medical school often requires!). But of course, whether it's a waste depends entirely on the person.

My wife has a master's degree in aeronautics and astronautics. Some FIRE naysayers believe she's wasting her knowledge and experience by retiring early, but my wife disagrees. She used her master's degree to boost her salary and work a successful career, but aeronautics and astronautics is not *who she is*. And once she got a taste of freedom after we quit our jobs and set sail in an RV, she was hooked.

She forgot all about her master's degree and lives every day enjoying the freedom to do anything she wants to do, customize every day so it works for her (and us!), and travel the country.

Note

1. "Retirees' Dilemma: Spend or Preserve?" EBRI (2021). `https://www.ebri.org/docs/default-source/fast-facts/ff.398.retireeprofiles.6may21.pdf?sfvrsn=abcd3a2f_6`.

Why You Should Never Retire Early

E arly retirement is great for some people but won't be right for everyone. There are specific types of people who probably shouldn't quit their jobs until they physically can't work any longer.

Let me introduce you to the early retirement *bell curve of happiness.*

Here's what a typical bell curve looks like:

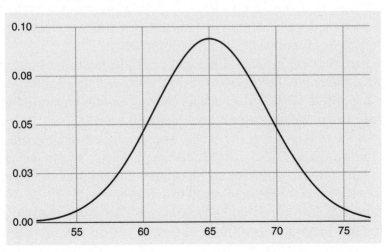

Think of the bell curve as a timeline.

At the beginning of the curve, our happiness is relatively low. We are working a job that we don't want to work. We're stressed out. Maybe overworked. Perhaps we hate our boss, you get the drill. We're unhappy with where we are and want to quit our jobs and do whatever we want for the rest of our lives. Sounds great, doesn't it?

Eventually, we hit FIRE. Yes! We can finally quit our job, and our happiness skyrockets (we're on our way up the left side of the curve). We're on top of the world. The alarm clock has already been smashed. We're getting up whenever we want, catching up on some of our favorite shows while plowing through that bag of Cheetos like it's going out of style, and teasing our friends on Sunday night because they will work the next day while we get to sleep in.

We're just living the life!

Then, something strange begins to happen. After a few weeks of early retirement, we feel a little antsy. Sure, getting up and doing nothing was great for a while, but now we realize there's more to life than just sitting around watching TV.

You might even admit to yourself at night, "I accomplished nothing today," getting slightly worried if tomorrow will be more of the same. More nothingness. More watching television or finding something to do just to keep busy.

Now, we're at the very top of the bell curve. Our happiness is no longer increasing. In fact, it's leveled off. You get more worried with each passing day that there's just nothing for you to do. Nothing to make you feel productive. To feel accomplished.

Then, that emotional rollercoaster barrels down the rightward slope of the curve. But unlike a real rollercoaster, this kinda sucks. Our happiness level is decreasing. We've become frustrated with nothing to do. We're getting on our spouse's nerves.

"Okay, this is not going well!" you finally admit. Eventually, you find your happiness right back where it began. You've just completed the full early retirement bell curve of happiness. And this is an accomplishment we don't want to achieve.

The goal is to turn that bell curve into a straight diagonal line where our happiness continues to elevate. To do this, we need to know why we're retiring early.

Hint: It can't just be "to stop working." For most of us, that isn't enough.

What Are You Retiring To?

If there's nothing else you take from this book, be sure to take this: know what you're retiring to, not just what you're retiring from.

We know what we don't like. It's our job. Or "working for the man." Or having to get up at 5 a.m., travel on the weekends, and have sleepless nights. Knowing what we don't want is easy.

The hard part is understanding what we do want.

Once we no longer have the demands of a full-time job, our entire day is free. That sounds like an incredible experience (and it can be!), but if you don't have hobbies or anything to do, you'll drive yourself (and your spouse!) crazy.

I am always busy. I love to write. I'm also on social media, teaching people about financial freedom. This is what I love to do, and so I do it. I'm almost never bored.

But if you have nothing to do in retirement, you'll find yourself right back at work.

Before making the decision to FIRE, you need to understand your purpose in life. What makes you tick? Without a job, why are you getting up in the morning? And at the end of the day, what will make you feel accomplished and productive?

For most of us, this takes time to figure out, so don't worry if you can't answer those questions just yet. It's okay.

However, I encourage you to consider those questions and figure this out if you dream of retiring early.

If you're unsure where to begin, here are a few ideas to get you started.

Reflect on your values: This is where "follow your passion" is good advice. Start by thinking about what is most important to you in life. Consider your core beliefs, passions, and things that bring you joy. Your purpose is often connected to the things that you value most.

Know your strengths: Think about the things you're good at and the skills that you have. Your purpose may be related to using those strengths to positively impact the world. Use early retirement to give back to your community and make a difference in the world.

Explore your interests: Consider what you enjoy doing in your free time, like nights and weekends. What hobbies or activities bring you the most fulfillment? Your true purpose might be right under your nose, and you don't even know it.

Experiment: Try new things and explore different opportunities (remember Habit #1 about saying yes?). You may discover your purpose through trial and error or through unexpected experiences. Exposure to new things can reveal our true purpose. But remember, your purpose can (and will) change, and you don't need to know every detail. If you're not sure, that's okay. In fact, that's what makes experimenting so much fun.

If you have no hobbies and nothing to do outside of working a full-time job, then you have no business retiring early.

However, financial independence should still be your goal. Being financially free gives you options, like quitting your job tomorrow if you don't like your boss. Or moving halfway across the world to a tropical island you also wanted to live on, as long as you have something to do once you are there.

Financial independence is still the goal, even if early retirement isn't.

What's Next?

Congratulations, you just got through the bulk of the book, but we're not done yet.

I'm giving you three bonus chapters that take you on an in-depth discussion about why credit cards can be a gold mine to save money (when you use them right), how to talk to your spouse about money, and debunking the worst piece of financial advice that I've ever heard. Chances are you've heard that piece of advice, too!

Don't skip these chapters. I included these bonuses for a reason, and they will help round out everything that you learned throughout this book.

Bonus Chapter: Why Credit Cards Are a Gold Mine

Credit cards get a bad rap in society, and for good reason. Did you know that the total debt in the United States as of 2022 is nearly $1 trillion?

How many zeros is that? Here you go: 1,000,000,000,000.

That's a ton of zeros, isn't it? That also represents a gigantic financial burden that most people carry on that easy-to-use piece of plastic they keep in their wallets or purse.

However, there's another side to credit cards that we often forget about. The perks that come from responsible credit card use make them a great way to spend money.

The keyword there is *responsible*.

If you can't use credit cards without amassing debt, you shouldn't use them because they are roadblocks to becoming a millionaire.

But if you can, they offer amazing benefits.

Benefits of Using Credit Cards

Rewards: Many credit cards offer rewards programs that allow you to earn points or cashback for every purchase you make. You can redeem these rewards for travel, merchandise, gift cards, or statement credits. In fact, Amazon lets you use some credit card points directly on their website as a payment method when you checkout.

Convenience: Credit cards are accepted at most merchants and can be used for online purchases, making them a convenient payment option instead of carrying around cash. It's also a safer way to pay; we'll discuss that in the fraud protection section.

Building credit: Using a credit card responsibly can help you build your credit score, which can be important for obtaining loans and credit in the future. It can also help lower your security deposit with utility companies or when renting a home.

Fraud protection: Credit cards offer better fraud protection than debit cards or cash. If your card is stolen or used fraudulently, you can report the unauthorized charges to your issuer and you will not be responsible for the charges. Unfortunately, there isn't much that you can do if your cash is stolen.

Purchase protection: Some credit cards offer purchase protection and warranties on the things you buy and will reimburse you for the cost of an item if it is lost, stolen, or damaged within a certain time frame after purchase. This makes many of those extended warranties that big-box stores try to sell unnecessary.

Travel perks: Some credit cards offer travel benefits, such as travel insurance, free checked bags, and airport lounge access, which can save money and make traveling more comfortable. I've been in several credit card lounges that have made long-distance travel much more tolerable.

It's important to note that the benefits of credit cards depend on the specific card you choose and how you use it. Read the terms and conditions carefully before applying for a credit card, and use it responsibly to avoid accruing high-interest debt.

How Credit Cards Get Hacked

Speaking of fraud protection, let's take a moment to talk about the different ways that criminals steal credit card information. Some of these hacks are pretty darn creative.

Credit card fraud typically involves the unauthorized access of a victim's credit card information through various means, such as phishing, skimming, or exploiting vulnerabilities in a website's security system. Here are some common methods hackers use:

Phishing: Hackers send fraudulent emails, texts, or make phone calls that appear from a legitimate source, such as a bank or a credit card company. The messages may contain a link to a fake website that looks similar to the real one. When the victim enters their credit card details on the fake website, the hacker can obtain and use the information for fraudulent transactions.

Skimming: Hackers install a skimmer on an ATM or a point-of-sale terminal such as a cash register. This device reads the magnetic stripe on the credit card and captures the information stored on it. The hacker can then use the information to create a cloned card and make unauthorized transactions. This happened to one of our credit cards at a gas station. Unfortunately, skimming works too well.

Malware: Hackers infect a target computer or mobile device with malware, a small software application that can capture credit card information when a computer user makes an online purchase. The malware may also steal login credentials or other personal information, making it especially dangerous.

Tip: A lot of malware gets distributed through email. Never open email attachments unless you know who it came from and were expecting it.

Social engineering: Smooth-talking hackers use social engineering tactics to trick victims into revealing their credit card information. For example, they may call the victim pretending to be a representative from a charity or organization asking for donations.

To protect yourself from credit card hacking, it is important to be vigilant and take appropriate security measures such as avoiding suspicious emails or websites, checking your credit card statements regularly (you should be doing this anyway as a part of your monthly expense tracking), and using strong passwords and security software on your devices.

Tip: If you get a call from a credit card company or bank, don't hesitate to hang up and call them back. You never know who is on the other end of that call. While writing this chapter, in fact, my wife got a call from someone who claimed to be from our credit card company investigating a fraudulent charge on our credit card. When they asked for personal information, my wife hung up, and I called the credit card company. Sure enough, nobody from the company had called us. We canceled that card immediately and had a new one issued. It's very easy to cancel a credit card. This was a social engineering type of hack that relied on the phone to extract personal information.

How to Use Credit Cards Wisely

By now, you understand how great credit card spending can be. Cards give you all kinds of protections and perks unavailable using cash or debit cards.

The key to making credit cards work for you is by using them in a responsible way. Let's devote the rest of this chapter to using credit cards correctly.

1. Use Credit Cards Only as a Convenience

Credit cards should only be used as a convenience, not as a way to spend money that you don't have. That means you aren't charging a $5,000 item to your card that you know you can't afford, assuming you'll pay it off next month (or the month after). This is how credit card debt happens, and this type of debt is extremely difficult to eliminate.

If you have credit card debt, make it a priority to squash those debts ASAP using the debt repayment techniques discussed in Habit #10.

2. Choose Credit Cards with the Best Perks

To get the most out of your credit card, pick the cards with the best credit card perks. For instance, some cards offer cash back at the end of the year, while others provide points that can be redeemed for travel-related purchases such as airline tickets, hotel stays, and rental cars.

Pay attention to bonus offers for many cards. These offers give a lot of additional points after spending a certain amount of money on the card within a specific time frame. For instance, you might get 60,000 bonus points after spending $4,000 on your card within the first three months of opening the card.

60,000 points? Score! But be careful. Don't fall into spending more money just to get the points. The math doesn't usually add up. Instead, spend the same amount of money you would ordinarily spend, but use the card offering the introductory points offer. In the end, you're spending the same amount. The only difference is the card that you're using at the register.

Note: "Credit card hacking" is a technique some use to exploit the perks, cash-back rewards, and bonus point offers on credit cards. The idea is to rack up as many points as possible with one credit card, then do the same with another, and so on. Expert credit card hackers might have 10 or 15 cards.

Though we aren't experts, my wife and I did some credit card hacking a few years before we quit our jobs to travel the country. We would apply for credit cards with the highest bonus reward points, spend the next couple of months using that card to meet the minimum spending requirement, then collect the points we redeemed for travel. That saved us hundreds of dollars with flights, rental cars, and hotel stays.

Fair warning: Credit card hacking is an advanced technique that requires attention to detail and staying on top of each credit card bill. If you are battling credit card debt or don't trust yourself not to overspend, using just one or two credit cards is probably the safer route until you get comfortable with responsible credit spending.

3. Pay Off the Card Every Month

This is nonnegotiable: If you can't pay off your card at the end of each month, then you're spending too much money. You need to pay off the credit card every month, which goes back to the first point of responsible credit card use. If you can't afford it in cash, you can't use a credit card.

Always, without exception, pay off that credit card every month.

To help you pay off your credit card every month, set up an automated bank transfer from your primary checking account to your credit card. You will set this up by logging into your credit card provider's website. This routine will run every month and pay off whatever your credit card balance is for that month. However, keep an eye on your balance to ensure you don't overdraft your bank account. Overdrafting your account means taking out more money than you have in the account.

For instance, if your credit card balance is $1,500, but you only have $1,300 in your bank account, then a $200 overdraft would occur if you tried to pay your credit card bill with that bank account. Banks typically charge $30 to $35 every time you overdraft your account, though some banks offer a limited window to replenish your account before overdraft fees happen.

Bonus Chapter: Why "Follow Your Passion" Is Bad Advice

"Follow your passion." It's advice I've heard all my life; chances are you have too. It's one of the worst pieces of advice regarding making money.

It sounds good, though, doesn't it? After all, we all want to love what we do for a living.

The problem with this advice? It's unrealistic for most of us, and it could hurt your career income potential.

For most of us, our passions don't pay the bills. Not like our strengths, anyway. Our passions tend to be more creative. More high-level. Our strengths, on the other hand, are often more practical and analytical. And while there are exceptions, most employers pay more for analytical-type jobs, not creative ones.

But that's not the only problem with the "follow your passion" advice.

Problem: It Assumes That Our Passions Never Change

If we set sail along a career trajectory based on our passions as late teenage people, we will likely find ourselves looking for a change later in life.

The fact is, for most of us, our passions change. Our life experiences alter our passions every year. And when that happens, we could find ourselves working a job that we no longer enjoy because our passions are different as 30-year-olds from what they were as 18-year-olds. Changing careers to reflect new passions is tough.

Think back to high school. What did you enjoy doing? Chances are you no longer do those things. Your exposure to life has formed new and improved passions today, and those new passions are the things you enjoy doing in your spare time. And 10 years from now, they might change again.

For instance, I love to write today (hence this book!), but I never enjoyed writing as a young person. I thought it was boring and uneventful. Through experience, I learned just how much wisdom can be spread through the written word.

Problem: It Makes It Seem as If Jobs Should Be Fun

First, let me get this out of the way: we should never work a job we hate—that's certainly no way to go through life or a career. But let's face it: jobs are not always fun. And we should never expect our jobs to be fun because when we do, we often find ourselves disappointed when they become stressful or difficult. And this is especially disappointing when we work a "passion" job because our passions aren't supposed to be stressful. They are supposed to be activities we do in our spare time, without worry about making money or pleasing bosses or customers.

For example, say you love art. I can barely draw a recognizable stick figure (this is true), but you are a maestro with the pen (or brush). You love to draw and decide to pursue a career in graphic design, assuming your passion for art will make that job easy and stress free. The problem? There's still the "jobbiness" aspect of a graphic design career that you can't escape. Like the impossible-to-meet deadlines. Toxic bosses. Unpaid overtime. Coworkers who just won't shut up about their spouse. Insanely annoying clients who don't know what they want, only what they *don't want.*

By the time you get home, the last thing you want to do is draw. It's your time to unwind from the day and think about other things until you're right back in the office again pursuing something that turned from your passion into a full-time job.

Problem: Full-time Jobs Destroy Passions

I alluded to this above, but let's go ahead and face this full-on: if we turn our passions into a full-time job, the not-so-nice elements of the job could destroy any passion we once had for it.

Raise your hand if you like performance reviews. Or the pointless meetings. How about sitting in uncomfortable cubicles? Does anyone enjoy those things?

There is a lot about jobs that most of us don't like. The last thing we want to do is associate something we enjoy with job-related activities that we don't.

My passion has always been photography. I worked at a camera store in high school and had my own photo darkroom in my parents' basement, where I developed my own film and made 8×10 prints. It was a lot of fun. And I still enjoy it because I chose not to make photography my career. Instead, I entered software engineering, a career field with demonstrably higher pay and better job opportunities.

Problem: Your Passions Are Not Always Your Strengths

Employers pay us a salary because we are good at performing a job they need to do. If you're good at math, maybe you're an accountant. Or if you're a great writer, perhaps you write technical manuals or edit manuscripts for publishers. But our passions, which in many cases are highly creative activities, are different, aren't they?

We may not be good at our passions, even though we enjoy doing those things. That's what makes them passions. We don't have to be good at them. We just need to enjoy doing them. For instance, there are far better photographers than I am. Better photo editors. Better equipment to use. And you know what? That's fine. I don't have to be the best photographer around to enjoy it. In fact, that makes me enjoy it even more. It's about me, not about impressing clients or magazine editors.

Our passions don't pay the bills like our strengths do.

Our strengths are what we are naturally good at, and our strengths tend to be more analytical. Disciplines such as math and science, problem-solving, marketing, and business are all desired skills in the marketplace. These are the skills that most employers look for. And these skills also result in the longest and highest-paid careers on average.

Problem: You Might Not Know Your Passion

Most of us choose a career path when we're young. We go to college, get a degree, and then enter the workforce ready to start making money. But what happens when we don't know what we are passionate about?

This happens more than you probably realize. Very often, passions are not necessarily readily apparent, especially at such a young age.

So "follow your passion" is bad advice. What should you do instead?

I encourage everyone to follow their *strengths*.

Our strengths are those we are naturally good at, almost without even trying.

Remember that jackass who got straight As in science class without even trying while you had to bust your butt to learn every little thing? Yeah, that's the kind of strength I'm talking about. And while these things can (and do) change over the course of a lifetime, they don't tend to change quite as rapidly or as fully as our passions.

I'm good at working with computers. Building websites and writing computer programs come naturally to me, so I chose a career aligned with that strength. And believe me, computers aren't my passion. I don't get up every morning and look forward to building my next computer. That just doesn't happen.

But my decision to follow that strength set me down a high-paying career path, helped me build wealth rapidly, and gave me time to pursue my passions on the side without having to worry about monetizing those passions.

In general, our strengths are easier to earn a living off. For instance, some of us are gifted marketers. Others are skilled at writing complex math algorithms. You might be a natural "people person," making you great at human resources. Employers worldwide are looking for these types of strengths and are willing to pay handsomely for skilled labor (in other words, you) to do them.

How many people are "passionate" about human resources? Probably not many. After all, who likes organizing mountains of paperwork, resolving employee disputes, and fielding petty grievances among their staff? Your HR director at work is good at what they do and earns a nice salary.

Following your strengths at the office means you can more fully embrace your passions at home without turning them into a source of full-time income. In other words, we shouldn't force our passions to pay the bills. Instead, we are free to pursue passions simply because we enjoy doing them.

And don't forget, most of us have a good idea of what we're good at, even at a very young age. Some of us are great at math or science. Others, language or history.

School makes it easy to determine what areas we are naturally gifted in, and by following our strengths instead of our passions, we can more easily pursue a career path that will likely set us up in a well-paying career field over the long term.

Bonus Chapter: How to Talk to Your Spouse about Money

Disagreements about money are the second leading cause of divorce, behind infidelity. For many couples, having the "money talk" is so intimidating that they just don't do it.

But this is a big mistake.

Before my wife and I achieved FIRE, we talked about money almost daily. After dinner, we took our two dogs for a walk around the neighborhood and discussed what we wanted our future to be like. We talked about everything, from our dream of traveling the country in an RV to how much money it would take to get us there.

We learned that I'm a more risk-tolerant person, and my wife was more risk-averse. I wanted to retire **right now**! My wife was a little more realistic.

Knowing the risk tolerance of the other person helped set real and pointed future expectations. My wife knew that I was prepared to quit virtually any time, while I knew my wife would prefer to work a little longer to ensure we retire with enough money.

In fact, I may have told her, "Honey, as soon as you think we have enough money to retire, let me know, and I'll put in my two weeks' notice that day."

These conversations are what shaped our post-work life. Knowing what our dreams looked like helped us work backward and map out the path to get there.

I know it won't be this easy for everyone. Our money decisions are highly emotional, and discussing your emotions with your spouse can be intimidating.

Here are ten ways to make talking money with your spouse easier:

Schedule a time to talk: Instead of surprising the other person (*"Honey, we really need to talk about all this spending. . ."*), set aside a specific time to discuss money. This way, you can prepare and avoid distractions or interruptions. Be sure to choose a time when both of you are calm and relaxed. Avoid times when either of you is stressed or in a bad mood. If you need to go out to dinner to avoid distractions at home, do it.

Be honest and transparent: When talking about money, it's important to be honest and transparent. Share your financial goals, fears, and struggles with your spouse. Discuss your income, expenses, and debt. Be clear about your financial situation and what you want to achieve. Give your spouse the same courtesy and listen when they talk.

Listen to your spouse: Effective communication involves active listening. Listen to your spouse's thoughts and concerns about money without interrupting or judging. Encourage them to share their ideas, hopes, and dreams. Acknowledge their views, even if you disagree. Remember, communication is a two-way street. It's okay not to see eye-to-eye on money decisions (in fact, that's common!). Recognizing where you differ and brainstorming ways to work past it is important.

Never blame or yell: Blaming or accusing your spouse of financial problems will quickly lead the conversation down an unhealthy path. Instead, focus on finding solutions together rather than on disagreements or pointing fingers. Avoid making assumptions or jumping to conclusions. Take responsibility for your actions, and work toward finding a solution. Blaming your spouse won't solve anything.

Establish joint goals: The only way you'll achieve your money goals is to get them out of your head and on the table. Discuss your financial goals and set a plan to achieve them together. Determine short-term and long-term goals, such as paying off debt, saving for retirement, buying a house, or even early retirement. Make a budget that reflects your financial goals, and stick to it.

Divide financial responsibilities: One person shouldn't need to assume the lion's share of the financial responsibilities. Instead, divide financial responsibilities based on your strengths and interests. For example, one spouse may be good at managing bills, while the other is good at investing. Be clear about who will be responsible for paying bills, managing investments, or saving for emergencies. Don't forget that financial automation can make bill pay, saving, and investing easy and straightforward.

Be open to compromise: Compromise is essential regarding money matters in a relationship. Be open to compromise and finding solutions that work for both of you. If both of you have very different dreams for your future, discuss how you can achieve them or tweak them to become your shared future dreams.

Seek professional help: There is nothing wrong with getting help from a qualified counselor or a financial planner if you and your spouse cannot make financial decisions. A financial planner or counselor can help you develop a plan to manage your finances and achieve your goals. They can also provide unbiased advice and support.

Be patient and persistent: Talking about money is an ongoing process. Building healthy and open communication about finances takes time, patience, and persistence. Be patient and persistent, even if the conversation is difficult. Remember that the goal is to work together toward a better financial future. You don't need to have everything figured out after the first time you sit down and talk money with your spouse. In time, the more you talk, the more likely you will find a middle ground.

Celebrate your wins: Finally, celebrate your successes together. When you achieve a financial goal or progress toward it, celebrate your success together (even if that means spending a little extra money). Acknowledge each other's efforts and accomplishments. Celebrating your successes will strengthen your relationship and motivate you to work toward your financial goals.

Conclusion

And, we're done!

I hope you enjoyed reading this book as much as I enjoyed writing it. Following these millionaire habits will help you get richer and more successful than you ever imagined possible. I've seen it happen with so many people.

The key is to be open to change and try new things. Don't give yourself a reason not to try. Instead, find the motivation to take money seriously and give these habits a legitimate try. Do it for your family. Do it for your future.

Here's a little something my wife and I learned along the way. Change is tough as hell. It's not easy to drastically alter how we live and spend our money. But the process's hardest part is when we start on this journey. Once we get the ball rolling, it gets easier. Every step makes the next step possible.

I didn't go from a heavy spender to financially independent overnight. It took years to accomplish. And so, don't expect this process to be easy, but understand that getting started is the biggest hump. Once you clear it, you're heading downhill.

I wrote this book because I have tremendous faith in you. I know that you can do this.

And I think you know that, too.

Acknowledgments

This book would not have been possible without my wife Courtney's help, patience, and understanding (and for humoring me along the way). Your unwavering belief in my dreams, endless encouragement, and patience throughout this writing journey have been immeasurable. Your love and understanding have fueled my determination, and I am forever grateful to have you by my side.

To my family, thank you for your constant support and understanding. Your love and encouragement have been instrumental in my pursuit of financial independence and writing this book. I am indebted to you for the sacrifices you have made and your belief in me.

I would like to sincerely thank my editor and publishing team for their invaluable work (it couldn't have been easy!). Your guidance, expertise, and tireless efforts have transformed my ideas into a coherent and impactful book. Thank you for your patience, dedication, and belief in the potential of *Millionaire Habits*.

I am grateful to my mentors and advisors, whose wisdom and guidance have shaped my understanding of wealth creation and personal development. Your insights and encouragement have been invaluable, and I am deeply grateful for your continued support.

My friends and colleagues, thank you for your unwavering support and encouragement. Your belief in me and encouragement throughout this journey have been a constant source of inspiration.

I am indebted to the countless individuals who have shared their stories and experiences with me, especially on social media. Your openness and willingness to share your knowledge and insights have enriched this book, and I am immensely grateful for your contribution.

Finally, I would like to express my gratitude to all the readers of *Millionaire Habits*. Your interest in this book and willingness to explore wealth-creation habits is humbling. I hope the ideas presented in this book will empower you on your journey toward financial abundance and personal fulfillment.

Thank you all for being a part of this incredible journey.

Sincerely,

Steve Adcock

About the Author

S teve Adcock is 42 years old and lives with his wife, Courtney, and two dogs in the desert Southwest. After working a 15-year career in information technology and aerospace engineering, respectively, Steve and Courtney sold their home, bought an Airstream RV, and hit the road, living full-time in their 200-square-foot "silver bullet" for three years. In 2019, they sold their Airstream and settled in a solar-powered off-grid home in the desert.

Along with Courtney's salary as a former rocket scientist (yes, an actual rocket scientist), their income, coupled with a low cost of living, allowed them to quit their jobs in their mid-30s.

Steve spends much of his time on social media and writing a rapidly growing newsletter called Millionaire Habits, available at millionairehabits.us.

Index